THE
FLOWER ARRANGER'S GARDEN

month-by-month

THE
FLOWER ARRANGER'S GARDEN
month-by-month

LEILA AITKEN

David & Charles

*To my delightful grandchildren, Lisa, Robert,
Isla, Leila, Susannah and wee Robbie*

A DAVID & CHARLES BOOK

Copyright © Leila Aitken 1995
First published 1995

Leila Aitken Has asserted her right to be identified
as author of this work in accordance with the Copyright
Designs and Patents Act 1988.

A catalogue record for this book is available from
the British Library.

ISBN 0 7153 0296 5

Colour illustrations by Avis Murray
Black and white illustations by Eva Melhuish
Photographs: All photographs by Jack Crombie except pp 2, 3, 6,
10–11, 36–7, 48–9, 60–1, 72–3, Clive Nichols; pp 57, 84–5, 113,
122, 124 Stuart Hamilton; pp116–17 Justyn Willsmore

Book design by Di Knapp

Typeset by ABM Typographics Ltd, Hull
and printed in Italy by New Interlitho SpA
for David & Charles
Brunel House   Newton Abbot   Devon

CONTENTS

INTRODUCTION

Every keen gardener can become a proficient flower arranger. Flower arrangement is a natural follow-on to growing your own plants and exactly the same skills go into making a flower arrangement that go into the making of a garden. In her book, *Wood and Garden* (1899), Gertrude Jekyll describes planning a flower border as 'not so difficult to create ... it is painting a picture with living plants'. This is flower arranging for the gardener, in a nutshell.

The flower arrangements in this book were all photographed at Greywalls on the East Lothian coastline. Greywalls, a crescent-shaped house designed by Edward Lutyens, has a garden strongly influenced by Gertrude Jekyll. It is a level garden, within high curving walls, and typical of her style of mixed formal and natural planting – hidden areas with garden 'rooms' enclosed by holly hedges, a rose garden bordered by lavender, theme borders in silver and white, as well as seasonal borders of exuberant herbaceous plants.

There is a pervading atmosphere of history and timelessness, both in the house and in the garden. In Victorian times, in houses like these, cutting flowers for the rooms was the sacred prerogative of the head gardener, who sometimes helped in the arranging. It seemed very appropriate, therefore, to be cutting flowers from the garden of one of the first floral artists, Gertrude Jekyll, to make arrangements for a book written with the object of encouraging every gardener to be a flower arranger.

AN ANALYSIS OF BEAUTY

An Analysis of Beauty is the name of a book published in the 18th century by William Hogarth. In it he mentions a lazy S-shaped curve and refers to it as 'the line of beauty'.

This then became known as the 'Hogarth Curve', and the mark of a good flower arranger was a well-shaped Hogarth curve. Other, less flowing and more geometric shapes followed, and in the sixties flower arrangements were stiff and somewhat uniform. Gradually this precise style of flower arranging lost popularity and a looser style gained ground. This led to an unstructured and sometimes haphazard style of arranging, whereby any jumble of flowers in an unrelated pot can be dubbed a flower arrangement.

Nowadays, the style generally accepted as most pleasing to the eye and enhancing the flowers and the surroundings is somewhere in between. It is a free style of arranging, blending colours and containers harmoniously, and takes the surroundings and the occasion into account. Flower arrangements for a church wedding, for example,

(opposite) *The lovely soft yellow flowers of* Argyranthemum *'Jamaica Primrose', seen here with* Hypericum androsaemum *and* Scabiosa ochroleuca, *are marvellous in arrangements.*
(below) *Greywalls was central to the creation of the arrangements in this book; its gardens provided the materials and its elegant rooms are ideal for display.*

mass arrangement

tend to be more formal and geometric than a posy on the supper table at home. The most popular shape for formal arrangements is still the triangle – the outline shape for wedding pedestals and the shape most used by florists. Other, abstract styles in flower arranging are also interesting and something you may come across if you join your local flower club.

So, although a regimented look to a flower arrangement is these days quite rightly despised, it is a help to have a picture of the general outline shape in your head before you start. The main outlines you will want to use are triangular, both symmetrical and asymmetrical, upright, L-shaped, mass, vertical and an inverted crescent.

ESSENTIAL EQUIPMENT

Basic, but inexpensive equipment is essential to the flower arranger. Keep it in a special flower cupboard or on shelves in the garage. Try to get all of the following:

Floral foam – a common trade name is oasis. It is sold in rounds and brick-sized blocks. Always have a couple of these large blocks handy – it is the most economical way to buy it as they can be cut to fit any container

Oasis tape – for taping around the block of foam and the dish, to keep the two securely together

Plastic oasis prong – known for some reason as 'frogs'. The foam is impaled on one of these to hold it in place in a shallow container, when it cannot be firmly wedged

Oasis fix – a very sticky, plasticine-type substance that fixes the plastic frog or oasis

A heavy metal pin holder – used to anchor branches or driftwood that are too heavy for the floral foam to support

Oasis saucers – plastic saucers (green is the best colour to buy, white is too noticeable)

Small secateurs and scissors – special flower scissors, with short curved points, make trimming foliage much easier once it is in an arrangement

Wire mesh netting – 2.5cm (1in), available in packs

A selection of florist's wires – reel wire is generally handy, keep also a couple of bundles of stem wire of different gauges.

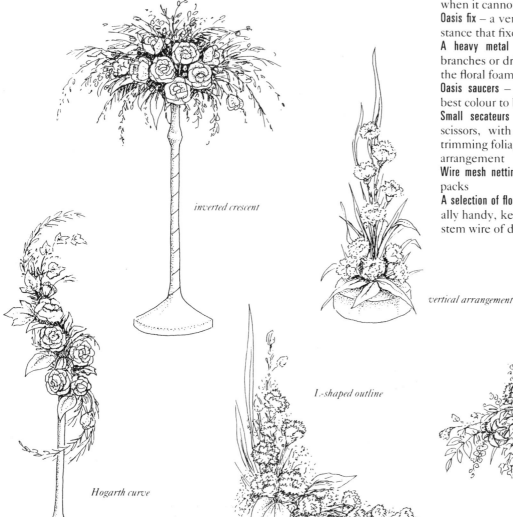

inverted crescent

vertical arrangement

Hogarth curve

L-shaped outline

triangular outline

COLLECTING CONTAINERS

You will not find a self-respecting flower arranger referring to, or even using, a vase! What you put your flowers in, in flower arranging terms, is NOT a vase. It is a 'container'. A container has to fulfil two functions – to hold the floral foam securely and above all to enhance the appearance of the flowers. The traditional flower vase, with a narrow base widening out at the lip, fulfils neither of these. Unfortunately, most churches have splendid brass examples of this kind of shape. It is very hard to make a soft outline of foliage when the vase shape holds stems upright and rigid which dictates the framework of the design.

Start now looking around and enjoy collecting containers that lend themselves to flower arranging and make the job easier. They include plates, goblets, urns, candlesticks, lamp holders, ceramic pots and tea pots. In this book the containers range from a cheap plastic dish to an expensive pottery elephant.

Shapes in containers

Shallow dishes are the easiest type of container for your first arrangement. The oasis is placed directly on a shallow pottery dish, as with the snowdrop arrangement on page 16. Look for flat trays or shallow, oval, round or kidney-shaped dishes. Special shallow dishes are now available for flower arranging that have a smaller dish fixed inside them, usually placed off-centre, of exactly the right size to take a round of oasis.

To hold oasis for an arrangement where the container will not be seen, you can buy inexpensive oasis holders from florists. Deep lids from coffee jars or saucers serve the same purpose. Use these also to hold water and wet oasis if a dish you want to use is too shallow, or when you don't want to place wet foam directly onto a surface – a silver tray for example.

Urn-shaped or water-pot containers are the next easiest shape to arrange. Collect these in several different shapes and sizes. 'Footed' containers, as they are known in the flower-arranging world, are the most satisfying containers to use because any raised arrangement looks light and delicate. So collect candlesticks, pedestals and footed containers.

Texture and colour of containers

One thing all containers should have in common is that they should be fairly plain. A highly ornamented or garishly coloured dish will detract from the flowers.

Choose the colour of your container to enhance your flowers. Leaf-green and dark green, earth-brown, terracotta and sludgy colours all improve the appearance of a flower arrangement.

My favourite container in this book is the large, green, glazed pot holding the garden annuals on page 85. That pot blends perfectly with any blossom, foliage or flowers that are arranged in it. Try this – cover the pot in the photograph with a small piece of white card to represent the pot. Immediately the white pot 'takes away' from the flowers.

The dull shine of most metals – copper, silver, pewter, steel and bronze – looks wonderful with most flowers. Metals can be used for a sophisticated arrangement as with the camellias (page 46), whereas the earthy, subdued, textural quality of wood enhances unsophisticated flowers such as the daffodils (page 24). You will enjoy discovering the effect that the texture, shape and colour of the container will have on different flowers. Look around and start your collection.

SEASONS AND MONTHS

Under average conditions, the terms 'early', 'mid' and 'late' season are used throughout this book to correspond to the following months:

SPRING
Early: March
Mid: April
Late: May

SUMMER
Early: June
Mid: July
Late: August

AUTUMN
Early: September
Mid: October
Late: November

WINTER
Early: December
Mid: January
Late: February

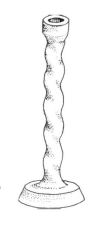

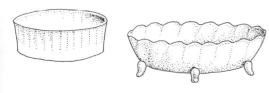

J A N U A R Y

The short, cold days make this the quietest month in the garden.
But every gardener is an optimist – the days lengthen almost
imperceptibly and our spirits rise as we begin to think about
getting out and starting to work in the garden again. Outside
work is minimal as this is usually the coldest month of the year.
But it is the month for constructive planning.
Most gardening magazines advise us to sit by the fire with a seed
catalogue. No true gardener ever does this. It may look as though
we are but in fact, we are off with our imagination, wandering
along lavish herbaceous borders, planting choice shrubs and
picking outsize sweet peas. The gardener and flower arranger is
also combining different shapes of foliage and flowers and
planning new colour schemes, moving blocks of colour around.
An evening with a seed catalogue can be very tiring! And is there
any other month when we so value the beauty of flowers? Every
year it comes as a total surprise to see the startling yellow heads of
the aconites and the fragile snowdrop heads that always look as
though they may lose their struggle through the crusted earth.
Small, delicate flowers like these do not lend themselves to formal
flower arranging, but the charm and beauty of each individual
flower can be shown to advantage if they are grouped in a simple
arrangement, rather than merely crammed into a jam jar!
The flower arranger needs more annuals and half-hardy annuals
for cutting than most gardeners, and this is the month to make the
selection and order the seeds, and also to map out an area where
they are to be grown. Late in the month is also an excellent time to
plant bare-rooted trees and shrubs as well as container-grown
plants, as long as there is no frost. Inevitably, the ritual task this
month is firming up trees and shrubs loosened by strong winds.

tasks
FOR THE
month

TINY PINKS
Try the tiny maiden pink (Dianthus deltoides) as an edging for a rose bed. Normally a rock garden plant, from early summer till autumn it is smothered with small red, pink or white flowers. Dianthus neglectus is also good, although more variable. The leaves form grey-green tufts and it starts to flower in midsummer with pale pink to deep crimson flowers.

GOOD ANNUALS FOR CUTTING AND ARRANGING

Arctotis
Argyranthemum (Chrysanthemum frutescens – Paris daisies)
Bartonia
Cornflower (Centaurea cyanus)
Cosmos
Crepis
Gaillardia
Gazania
Gypsophila
Larkspur
Lavatera 'Pink Beauty'
Limonium
Love-lies-bleeding (Amaranthus)
Moluccella laevis
Night-scented stock (Matthiola bicornis)
Nicotiana alata
Iceland and annual poppies
Rudbeckia
Scabious
Snapdragon (Antirrhinum)
Straw flower (Helichrysum)
Sweet pea (Lathyrus odoratus)
Zinnia (particularly the lime-green variety 'Envy')

PLANNING

GROWING SHRUBS

A flower arranger's garden is planted according to different priorities from the garden next door. A constant supply of flowers and foliage for cutting is needed to enjoy in the house and to make flower arrangements to give to friends, or to help out at the local church, hotel or hospital.

If you are a keen flower arranger with only a small garden, my advice is – grow shrubs! A branch or two of a flowering shrub brought indoors to be displayed in an unusual container against a plain wall has more decorative or dramatic effect and contributes more to a room than a bunch of flowers alone. But limited space is not the only reason for concentrating on shrubs. The main reason is that flower arranging uses a combination of different leaf shapes, foliage textures and plant forms. The aim is to combine these in as pleasing a way as possible as a background to any flowers. It is the *choice* of foliage that is the starting point of a display and it is this which makes every flower arrangement different from the next. The arrangement you make using the fresh green growth of spring, for example, will be quite unlike the arrangement made from the same foliage

in autumn, and it will call for a completely different choice of flowers. Also – you can buy flowers from a florist all year round but you *cannot* buy a wide selection of foliage.

THE IDEAL GARDEN

In an ideal world, the flower arranger's garden would have a large border of mixed shrubs that includes many flowering species, some variegated shrubs and some evergreens to give shape to the border during the winter as well as providing foliage for arranging. It would also have a special border for cutting, tucked away from the main garden area, that contains the annuals no flower arranger would want to be without and a well-stocked, old-fashioned type of herbaceous border containing a choice of plants for dried arrangements.

Lastly, a spacious potting shed to hold the awesome collection of equipment you will amass.

Back to reality. Most of us have to settle for a compromise and establish our priorities. For flower arrangers these are **shrubs** as the first priority, **annuals** next and **herbaceous plants** last. It is mostly herbaceous plants or greenhouse plants that are available from the florist. Delicate annuals and branches of blossom and flowering shrubs are not.

ROSES AND ANNUALS

There are two areas of the garden where I would not compromise: a bed given over entirely to **roses** (apart from edging plants), and a part of the garden devoted to **annuals**, both hardy and half-hardy, for picking.

Annuals have some of the same attributes as wild flowers in that they bring a special quality of lightness and charm to a flower arrangement. The cottage garden type of hardy annual such as Pot marigold (*Calendula*), candytuft (*Iberis*), *Godetia* and love-in-a-mist (*Nigella*) are the least sophisticated of flowers and harmonise well together in informal posies.

Half-hardy annuals, such as cosmos, gazania and rudbeckia, have more sophistication and blend into any arrangement, with any type of plant.

Most gardeners enjoy trying a few new varieties of annuals each year. In a small garden you have to tuck them between established plants, but if you have the space, you can allocate them their own special area. This way you can pick what you need for special occasions and for drying when flowers are at their peak without spoiling the display in the garden.

SITING A BORDER FOR ANNUALS

Annuals are the 'children' of the garden. Given the right conditions they blossom; in adverse conditions they sulk. Most annuals are not demanding but their position in the garden is paramount for getting good results – plenty of flowers over a long period. They need the sunniest site in a sheltered area to protect them from cold winds.

The shape of the flower

bed is, to some extent, dictated by the site. If you are growing annuals for cutting in a secluded or hidden part of the garden, the shape of the bed should be functional. If you have any choice, restrict the depth of the border. Position shorter plants to the front and edge so that you can cut the tallest plants at the back without damaging those at the front as you reach over.

If you have plenty of space, a double border with a path down the centre looks good, gives a wonderful walk-way through the annuals at the height of the summer and allows for easy picking. As with a single border, plant low-growing subjects at the front.

If the flower border can be seen from the house, site it at right angles to it so that the view is along the massed ranks of flowers rather than face on. In this case do not restrict yourself to annuals; include evergreen shrubs, bulbs and foliage plants at intervals to keep the interest during the winter.

The ideal site has a warm stone wall as a background, but a fence or hedge is the next best thing. Sweet peas, hollyhocks, giant larkspur, foxgloves, sunflowers, the giant thistle (*Onopordum*) and annual climbers such as nasturtium (*Tropaeolum*), thunbergia and convolvulus can be grown in its shelter.

SOIL FOR ANNUALS

For garden annuals, the soil is not quite as important as the site because annuals are in the ground for such a short time. Elaborate or deep preparation of the soil is not necessary. Any well-drained garden soil will do. Better results are obtained from slightly sandy soils, which warm up quickly, than from heavy or clay soils, which

obstruct the run of the fine roots.

Identify your soil

There can be more than one type of soil in different areas of your garden, and certainly two completely different soils in the same village less than a mile apart. My own garden, next to the sea, was initially almost pure sand. Less than a mile inland there are far more difficult conditions – gardens of very heavy clay.

Soil is a living medium made up of ground-down rock particles and organic matter. There are three layers: the base layer of rock, then the subsoil and the top layer of soil. This layer of topsoil varies in thickness in different localities – the thicker the layer, the more fertile the soil and the conditions for growing plants.

The original rock determines whether the soil is acid, alkaline or somewhere in between. Soils derived mostly from limestone are alkaline. Soils

derived mostly from granite are acid. But most soils are a mixture and it is best to test them with a soil test kit from a hardware store.

CHOICE OF PLANTS

There is a wide choice of annuals for flower arranging. Some seed catalogues indicate those that are particularly good for cutting, and they often include lists of everlasting flowers that are easy to grow in the annual border. For flower arranging choose single rather than mixed colours.

We all grow our own favourites, in colours we find agreeable, ignoring others. For instance, in my garden you will have to look hard to find a purple flower! One person's choice is not the same as another's, but there are some annuals that are more rewarding than others for arranging – they last better in water and harmonise more readily with other flowers and foliage.

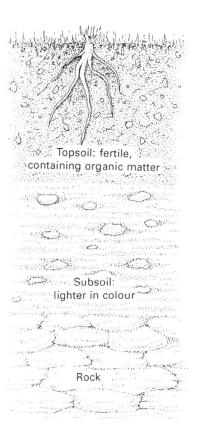

Topsoil: fertile, containing organic matter

Subsoil: lighter in colour

Rock

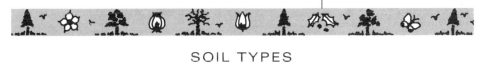

SOIL TYPES

	Structure	Drainage	Fertility	Cultivation	Temperature
SANDY					
	Will only hold together when wet	Free-draining because of its open texture	Hungry, usually low in food reserves as plant food quickly washes through the soil	Light and easy to work, even when wet	Warms up early in spring, hot and dry in summer and needs frequent watering in hot weather
CLAY					
	Cakes hard and cracks when it becomes too dry	Badly drained because it holds too much water and too little air	Food reserves are good, added plant food is contained and gives lasting improvement	Heavy and difficult to work, especially under wet conditions	Slow to warm up, not suitable for early planting

plants

OF THE

month

EARLY DELIGHTS

My favourite occupation in mid-winter is to go round the garden and find the first snowdrops, showing a little white on spear-like buds. In a mild winter, it is possible to find one or two almost open flowers from sheltered areas. Failing that I lift a clump of snowdrops, soil and all, and pot it up to bring into the house where they open up beautifully. Replant them as soon as the flowers fade.

COMMON SNOWDROP
Galanthus nivalis

Justifiably called the 'harbinger of spring', it seems the snowdrop will grow anywhere for anybody. It can, however, be surprisingly difficult to establish on a dry soil. A woodland plant, it prefers moist shade and looks at its best in drifts under deciduous trees.

type	Bulb
flowers	Pendant, white, bell-shaped, made up of three large and three small petals tipped with green in mid- to late winter
foliage	Linear grey-green
height	10–15cm (4–6in)
planting	In early autumn, 5–8cm (2–3in) deep, in groups or drifts
position	Partial shade, any aspect, thrives in open woodland
soil	Fertile, moist soil
care	Allow foliage to die down naturally
propagation	Divide crowded clumps and replant immediately after flowering
varieties for flower arranging	*G. n.* 'Flore Plena' has double flowers; the single *G. elwesii* grows taller than the common snowdrop, up to 30cm (12in), with larger leaves

 ## CHINESE WITCH HAZEL
Hamamelis mollis

This plant can be spectacular, with prolific clusters of fragrant yellow flowers on bare branches in the depths of winter. Seen against a pewter-grey winter sky, it is especially superb. But if it does not like its soil and situation, it may be a dismal sight.

type	Hardy, deciduous flowering shrub
flowers	Cluster of spidery strap-shaped petals in mid-winter
foliage	Coarse, not useful for flower arranging
height	3m (10ft)
planting	In autumn or spring
position	Sun or semi-shade, sheltered from cold winds
soil	Well-drained peaty, acid soil
care	Incorporate leaf mould or peat to retain moisture during the summer
propagation	Not easy to propogate. Buy a container-grown shrub from a nursery
varieties for flower arranging	Japanese witch hazel *(H. japonica)* has yellow flowers with a slight reddish tinge. Flowers a few weeks later than *H. mollis*

CORKSCREW HAZEL

Corylus avellana 'Contorta'

This is a shrub to grow for fun. Known as Harry Lauder's walking stick, the curiously curled and convoluted branches are superb for modern flower arranging and, without their leaves, are a satisfying sight against a winter sky. I do not like this shrub in summer at all. The leaves are crumpled and look as though they are victims of a fungal attack. So, although it is a 'must' for the flower arranger, choose its position in the garden carefully.

type	Hardy, deciduous shrub
flowers	Small, inconspicuous flowers and yellow catkins in mid- to late winter. Nuts borne in clusters in mid-autumn
height	Slow grower, up to 6m (20ft)
planting	Mid-autumn to early spring
position	Open and sunny
soil	Any well-drained garden soil
care	Protect from cold winds in a severe winter. Collect nuts as they begin to harden and turn brown
propagation	Layer established shrubs in the autumn

WINTER ACONITE

Eranthis hyemalis

A cheerful, golden-yellow flower not rising far above the soil, which, once established, will spread satisfyingly. As with the yellow crocus, birds can sometimes decimate the crop.

type	Hardy, tuberous-rooted perennial
flowers	Shiny, buttercup-yellow with deeply cut ruffs of green bracts in mid- to late winter
foliage	None as such. The stems are bare with the flowers supported by a ruff of lime-green leaves
height	10cm (4in)
planting	Late summer 2.5cm (1in) deep in groups 8cm (3in) apart
position	Sun or partial shade under deciduous trees or shrubs
soil	Moist, fertile soil
care	Winter aconite are sometimes difficult to establish in sandy soils that lack moisture, but they need no special care
propagation	Undisturbed plants naturalise and seed themselves. Or lift, divide and replant immediately after flowering
varieties for flower arranging	Not really an arranger's flower in the true sense – but who can resist bringing this cheerful little flower inside on a bleak winter day?

TASSEL BUSH

Garrya elliptica

Not the most attractive of evergreen shrubs, but popular with flower arrangers because of their long greeny-grey catkins. The male plants are the most attractive with the longest catkins.

type	Evergreen, quick-growing, bushy shrub
flowers	Catkins with yellow anthers late winter to early spring
foliage	Ovate, grey-green, leathery leaves
height	4m (12ft)
planting	In spring
position	Sunny, enjoys the shelter of a wall
soil	Tolerates most soils
care	Protect for the first winter
propagation	By semi-ripe or heel cuttings in late summer, or by layering in late autumn
varieties for flower arranging	*G. e.* 'James Roof' has very long catkins

practical project *1*

'HOPE AND ECSTASY'

YOU WILL NEED

An oasis frog
Oasis fix
Small round of oasis, cut down to 5cm (2in) deep
Very small black or clear plastic cylindrical container, such as the top of an aerosol spray can or a 35mm film container

NEUTRAL BLACK
Black is a good basic colour – it doesn't draw attention to the container or dominate the flowers. Try the effect of putting a bunch of snowdrops in a brightly coloured or busily patterned small vase. You realise at once that the flowers lose out, because the delicacy of the snowdrop is eclipsed by the vase.

Like aconites, snowdrops are not suited to formal arrangements. This is a very simple yet effective way to arrange and enjoy them – grouped under the branches of a shrub as though they were still growing. The twigs should curve and reach upwards and outwards, with the snowdrops in clusters and the ivy trailing naturally at the base.

MATERIALS

The container
A kidney-shaped shallow dish in black

Foliage
Corkscrew hazel *(Corylus avellana)* 'Contorta'
Chinese witch hazel *(Hamamelis mollis)*
Ivy *(Hedera helix)*
Moss (gathered in flat clumps from a lawn or path)

Flowers
Snowdrops

■ Fix a small piece of oasis fix to the base of the frog, press it to the left side of the DRY dish. Impale the soaked oasis firmly on top. Or, look for a shallow dish with a smaller dish fixed inside, specially made to fit a round of oasis foam (fig 1a).

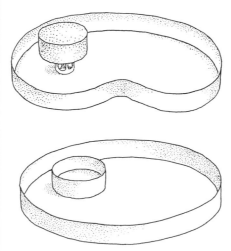

■ Insert a contorted branch of corkscrew hazel to the back and a shorter branch curving towards the front and to the right. Add three or four twigs of Chinese witch hazel following this outline (fig 1b).
■ Place a small group of snowdrops with a few of their leaves in the plastic container to the

right and in front of the branches and a second pot just at the base of the twigs.
■ Conceal the pots, oasis and base of the dish with damp moss. Add trails of ivy to break the hard outline of the rim of the dish (fig 1c).

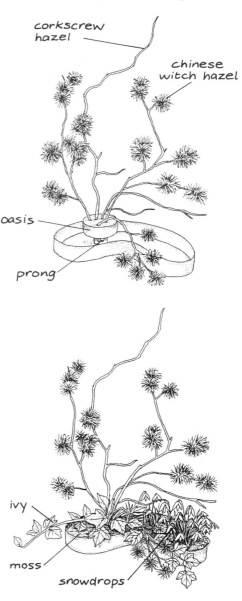

corkscrew hazel

chinese witch hazel

oasis

prong

ivy

moss

snowdrops

TIP

■ *A flower always looks best arranged as it grows. For example, gladioli look superb reaching up as the central column in a large arrangement, but look awkward and stiff when made to hang out stiffly to the sides* ■

The aconite is the first flower of the year and, unless we bring the glossy yellow heads indoors, they are enjoyed only briefly in passing as we scuttle past, heads down against the weather. Even a very small child can appreciate the beauty of flowers. The first spontaneous attempt at picking them is usually a fist full of flower heads that can only be saved by floating them in a saucer of water. This simple flower arrangement is merely one step removed from that.

Floating the heads in water is the best way to appreciate aconites. The green ruff of the bracts holds the yellow heads from the water showing the inner circle of fluffy yellow stamens. Floating candles can be added.

MATERIALS

The container
A cheap, clear plastic shallow bowl which, when filled with water, resembles solid glass. It is slightly irregular in shape which helps to give the impression of a pool of water, but any oval or round clear glass plastic dish will do.

Foliage
Tassel bush (*Garrya elliptica*)
Ivy (*Hedera helix*)

Flowers
Aconites

■ Place the heavy pin holder to one side of the dish (fig 2a). Cut a well-shaped branch of garrya with long catkins. Remove excess lower 'branches' and foliage to give a nicely-shaped

'tree' and also to display the catkins. Press the branch onto the pin holder. Group the stones around the pin holder to conceal it.
■ Fill the dish with water, almost to the rim. Float the candles, well apart and the aconite heads around them. Trail sprays of ivy over the stones and into the water (fig 2b).

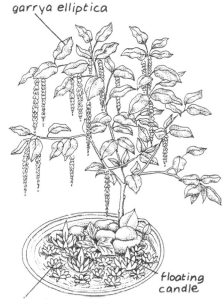

garrya elliptica

floating candle

aconite

practical project 2

'TRANQUILITY'

YOU WILL NEED

A metal pin holder (see basic flower arranging equipment, page 8)
A few attractive, coloured stones to disguise the pin holder
Floating water-lily candles

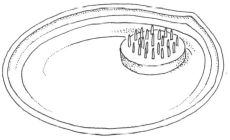

NOTE

■ *OUTDOORS INDOORS You can also dig up the aconites, tubers and all, pot them and bring them indoors. Then return them to the garden when the flowers fade. They will flower again the following year* ■

FEBRUARY

Now we begin to feel that winter is on its way out. We long for warmer days to spend time in the garden, and every burst of sunshine is an incentive to get out and start pruning, sowing, tidying and, on suitable days, planting. To me, planting this early is one of the chief joys of gardening. There is a tremendous thrill in planting a rose now. Almost at once the buds begin to lengthen, then show green and burst open to show tiny leaf tips. By late spring there is the incredible bronze-green of the new foliage, and midsummer the exquisite, delicate petals of the rose. Whatever the weather this month, there is always some blossom. The sunshine-yellow, cotton-wool clusters of Chinese witch hazel on its bare branches are breathtaking against a leaden blue-grey sky. Both Chinese witch hazel and viburnum species withstand appalling weather conditions and bloom against all odds throughout the coldest months of the year. To see the tiny pink blossoms of Viburnum bodnantense 'Dawn' in the cold light of the morning arouses all kinds of emotions – hope, reassurance, elation. No flower arranger can resist bringing a few twigs indoors. They prefer the outdoor chill of winter and will not last long, but they cheer up the home – even if only for a few days. It is a good idea to get any necessary pruning done early in the month, so you do not cut its home from beneath its feet. The great thing about being a flower arranger is that we seldom need to spend long hours on the 'cutting back' work in the garden. Much pruning of shrubs is done incidentally. As a flower arranger with a pair of secateurs in search of foliage or blossom for an arrangement one obviously cuts a branch so that the shape of the shrub is improved, or from a shrub that needs to be pruned anyway.

tasks

FOR THE

month

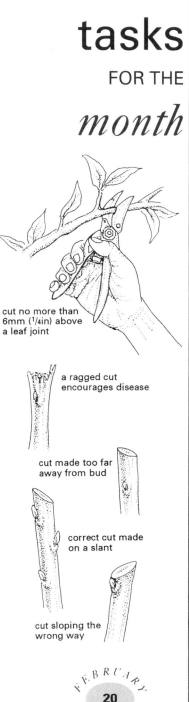

cut no more than
6mm (¹/₄in) above
a leaf joint

a ragged cut
encourages disease

cut made too far
away from bud

correct cut made
on a slant

cut sloping the
wrong way

CHECKLIST

- Check all your shrubs for pruning
- Trim evergreen shrubs
- Start growing half-hardy annuals from seed indoors
- Sow sweet peas indoors

MAINTENANCE

PRUNING

After a severe winter the majority of ornamental trees and shrubs will need a little light trimming to improve their appearance. Dead or wind-damaged twigs and distorted, frost-damaged leaves need to be removed. The main pruning in the garden is carried out in spring and, if you understand the logic behind it, it is quite straightforward. You are pruning for the **health** of the shrub, cut out the 3 D's – dead, diseased and damaged wood – to admit light and air; for the **shape** of the shrub – cut out branches that spoil the balanced shape or are unsightly, crossing or overcrowded; for **decoration** – prune to encourage flowering with larger blooms, or improved foliage and coloured stems.

The best time for pruning

Although light pruning can be done at any time of year, main pruning of deciduous shrubs should be done at a specific time:

- Shrubs that flower on new shoots, that is, this season's growth, in midsummer, for example the butterfly bush (*Buddleia*), are pruned back to leave 2-3 buds of last year's branches and are cut back in early spring before growth starts.
- Shrubs that have just finished flowering over the

winter or *will* finish flowering this month or next, such as forsythia, are pruned immediately after flowering. Those branches that have borne blooms are cut back to a bud near a junction with the main branches.

- It is important to identify the shrub *precisely* as this is only a general guide. Look up the shrub in an encyclopedia on gardening to check the time of year to prune it. For example, some varieties of *Berberis* are pruned differently from others, and the deciduous Californian lilac (*Ceanothus*) is treated differently from the evergreen variety.
- Evergreen shrubs only need trimming to shape and to remove unwanted branches in the spring. Don't be in a hurry to remove these – they

NOTE

- *Removal of entire branches will thin out the shrub and produce a laxer, more open shrub, with longer branches suitable for flower arranging. Light pruning, that is just removing the ends of the branches, stimulates the buds below to produce clusters of shoots. It produces a denser shrub with shorter branches – not what flower arrangers want*

may be useful in a flower arrangement later.

- Shrubs grown for the colour of the stems and not the flowers, such as dogwood (*Cornus alba*) with its red branches and *Cornus stolonifera* 'Flaviramea' with its yellow stems, should be cut down to just above the ground in late spring. New shoots of a more intense colour appear from the base.

Pruning established shrubs

- Sharp secateurs are essential to cut the stem cleanly without a split, which would encourage die-back and disease. Long-handled pruners are a boon for high branches and trees, so also is a shaped pruning saw for very thick branches.
- Choose a bud, a leaf joint or another branch from which new growth can be made. The cut should be no more than 6mm (¹/₄in) above the bud. Excess growth left above the pruning cut will die – it looks unsightly and encourages disease.
- Make the cut on a slant, sloping *away* from the bud, to allow rain to run off. Slanting the wrong way may result in die-back disease. If there are two leaf joints, opposite each other, the cut will have to be made straight across.
- The harder the shrub is pruned, the more growth it will produce. An unevenly balanced shrub can be shaped up by pruning it hard on the weak side, not, as you might expect, by pruning the heavier growth.

PROPAGATION

GROWING HALF-HARDY ANNUALS FROM SEED

There are two kinds of annuals, **hardy** and **half-hardy**. The seed packet will tell you which type a particular flower is. **Hardy annuals** can be sown direct into prepared ground when the soil has warmed up after the winter (see page 42). They will flower in summer. **Half-hardy annuals** are tender and are started off in pots or seed trays indoors or in a greenhouse, in early spring. They are planted out in late spring to flower in summer.

Sowing half-hardy annuals indoors

You can get by quite easily without a heated greenhouse for growing annuals but, if you have one, it gives them the best possible start for both germination and growing on. The next best thing is an electric propagator for germination and a cold greenhouse for growing them on.

Seeds need warmth, moisture and air to germinate and these conditions can be fulfilled in the home, using warm airing cupboards and window sills. A problem may arise later, in the growing on. If you sow the seeds too early, they will have to remain on the window sill for too long and may become 'leggy', due to lack of good light. So start the seeds off in the warmth of the home but, as soon as possible, give them full light – either in a cold greenhouse, cold frame, conservatory or on a window sill with good light but out of direct sunshine.

Compost

Choose a special seed-sowing compost from a garden centre. **Loam-based compost**, such as proprietary seed and potting composts, made up from a mixture of loam, soil, sand and peat. **Soil-less compost** containing peat or peat and sand mixtures. The peat in some composts is partially substituted by pulverised bark and the sand is replaced by vermiculite or perlite. Coir is a coconut fibre that is used as a substitute for peat in some soil-less composts.

My personal choice is always the seed and potting compost. Soil-less compost, although it gives excellent results and is light and clean to handle, can be difficult to re-wet if you allow it to become too dry. Whichever you choose, use the same type in the potting compost when the seedlings are large enough to be pricked out.

Useful equipment

There are four aids to seed sowing which I wouldn't be without:

■ a strip of wood (actually a piece of floor board), cut exactly to the width of a seed tray, which has a small block nailed to the top to use as a handle. This levels the compost quickly and cleanly.
■ an ordinary kitchen sieve allows a thin sprinkling of compost to fall through over very small seeds.
■ a square washing up bowl, slightly larger than a seed tray. Half fill this with water and stand the filled trays of compost in it to absorb the correct amount of water.
■ a small hand mist sprayer, used to keep the top of the compost moist and to spray the very tiny seedlings

Sowing half-hardy annuals

■ Fill a clean seed tray to within 1cm (½in) of the rim. Level it and firm gently.
■ Pour the seed from the packet into your hand and gently sprinkle seed very thinly and as evenly as possible over the surface of the compost. Mix very fine seed with sand to make this job easier.
■ Through a fine sieve, shake a very fine layer of compost over the seed (the smaller the seed the finer the layer).
■ Stand the tray in water to about half way up the sides. Remove from the water when the compost is evenly moist.

■ Cover the tray with a sheet of glass or clear plastic and cover this, in turn, with newspaper. The paper gives shade on sunny days and conserves moisture.
■ Maintain a temperature of 13–24°C (55–75°F). Consult the seed packet for the exact temperature needed. When the seedlings emerge remove the covering and keep them away from strong sunlight. Keep them moist and, when they have two leaves and are large enough to handle, transplant them into new compost (see page 28).

SWEET PEAS

Sweet peas are annuals and not difficult to grow. Buy your seed from specialist growers, though more expensive the results are much better.

Sowing sweet peas

■ Coat the seeds with seed dressing. This helps prevent the seed rotting in the compost, aids germination and also gives a strong root system.
■ Speed up germination of black-seeded varieties by chipping the seed coat with a sharp knife on the opposite side to the 'eye'. White, brown, and wrinkled varieties must not be chipped. If you find it difficult to handle the knife blade and slippery seed together, file the seed with a nail file to get through the hard coating.
■ Sow in individual, narrow, deep containers, such as proprietary sweet pea tubes or rolled tubes of newspaper. This way the roots grow strongly downwards and, as the plant, container and all are planted, it avoids root disturbance.
■ Once they are growing strongly, nip out the growing tip of the original seed growth to encourage the formation of side shoots.

NEGLECTED SHRUBS
Evergreen flowering shrubs that have become overgrown and misshapen through neglect, can be cut hard back at the end of this month, and given a top dressing of bonemeal and a mulch of peat or composted bark (see page 62). This is also very successful with neglected deciduous shrubs – spindly mock orange (philadelphus), laurel (aucuba), pernettya and hebe can all be drastically treated in this way. It means, however, that no blossom will be produced until the following year.

DISTRESSED SEEDS
The latest thinking, and the procedure advocated by some sweet pea growers, is that sweet pea seeds should not be soaked prior to sowing. Soaked seeds become distressed and germination levels are reduced.

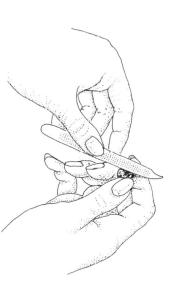

plants
OF THE
month

VIBURNUM
Viburnum × bodnantense

This shrub always steals upon us when we least expect it. In bad weather, when pottering around the garden has been curtailed, it can be breathtaking to come across the bare branches sprouting little bundles of pink blossom. This shrub should be planted more often as it is frost resistant and a very cheering sight on a grey winter's day.

type	Deciduous, upright shrub
flowers	Clusters of white-flushed, rosy-pink flowers, borne on stiff naked stems in winter. Sweetly scented
foliage	Ovate, toothed. Appears after the flowers, not useful in flower arranging
height	3m (10ft)
planting	Mid-autumn to early spring
position	Sheltered from cold winds and where early morning sun will not damage young flowers after frost
soil	Well-drained, moist soil. Thrives in chalky soil
care	Remove dead wood after flowering in spring
propagation	By semi-hardwood cuttings in late summer under glass. Can also be layered in autumn
varieties for flower arranging	V. × bodnantense 'Dawn' is a hybrid between V. farreri and V. grandiflorum and is hardy and frost resistant

CONVOLVULUS
Convolvulus cneorum

This small shrub is often found in old herb gardens. Today you may have to search for it at larger plant nurseries. It is a choice plant, grown for its wonderful soft, grey foliage rather than for its flowers. On a sunny day the leaves look silver, and they last well in water.

type	Half-hardy, evergreen, small shrub
flowers	Pink-tinged buds opening to white flowers, 2.5cm (1in) across, late spring to early autumn
foliage	Narrow, silver-grey, lanceolate leaves that look wonderful in the sunshine
height	60cm (24in)
planting	In spring
position	Sunny, sheltered
soil	Well-drained ordinary soil
care	Protect in wet, cold weather with a cloche
propagation	By heel cuttings in mid- to late summer

DOUBLE DAFFODILS
Narcissus – double cultivars

The yellow trumpet flower of Wordsworth's poem should, more correctly, have been described as narcissus, although there were not the number of narcissus hybrids then that there are now. The large trumpet daffodil is the essence of spring. From early winter onwards it is also plentiful in the shops. The flower arranger would do better to grow some of the double daffodils. There are dozens of wonderful double varieties available from specialist bulb nurseries. By careful selection of different flowering times you can prolong the daffodil season by several weeks. Pick double varieties just before they are fully open, as the heads are heavy and easily blown over in a strong wind.

type	Deciduous bulb
flowers	Golden-yellow, concentric circles of petals late winter to late spring, depending on variety and climate
foliage	Linear, up to 2.5cm (1in) wide
height	38–45cm (15–18in)
planting	In early autumn
position	Sun or light shade
soil	Fertile, well-drained soil
care	Allow the leaves to die down completely and feed the bulb before removing them
propagation	When overcrowded, narcissus will be 'blind', that is produce leaves only. Lift the bulbs and remove the small offsets. Replant bulbs and offsets at correct planting distance and sprinkle some bonemeal at the roots
varieties for flower arranging	'Golden Ducat' has double flowers, deep yellow throughout; 'Irene Copland' has Camellia-type flowers, cream and yellow petals interspersed; 'Tahiti' large yellow petals with smaller orange-red petals at the centre

PITTOSPORUM
Pittosporum tenuifolium

A 'must' for flower arranging. Although not absolutely hardy, no other evergreen shrub has the delicacy of its wavy-edged leaves. Given a modicum of shelter, it grows strongly and in mild coastal areas it is often used for hedging.

type	Half-hardy evergreen
flowers	Small and insignificant, dark

purple in late spring

foliage	Delightful, light green with wavy edges on thin, pliable black stems
height	Up to 4m (12ft)
planting	Mid- to late spring
position	Sunny, sheltered
soil	Well-drained fertile soil
care	Tends to grow straggly. Cut branches for arrangements to encourage a balanced shape
propagation	By semi-ripe heel cuttings in midsummer
varieties for flower arranging	*P. t.* 'Silver Queen' is silver-grey with variegated foliage; *P. t.* 'Garnettii' has rounded leaves, irregularly edged with cream

ELAEAGNUS
Elaeagnus pungens 'Maculata'

This shrub has such a shiny, varnished appearance that it can look unreal. It is a wonderful standby for the flower arranger at all seasons of the year.

type	Hardy, evergreen shrub
flowers	Inconspicuous, silvery flowers in mid- and late autumn
foliage	Ovate, leathery leaves, glossy green splashed with mustard-yellow
height	3m (10ft)
planting	In autumn or spring
position	Does equally well in sun or shade
soil	Any ordinary soil
care	Remove any shoots produced that are not variegated as soon as they appear
propagation	By hardwood cuttings in late autumn
varieties for flower arranging	*E.p.* 'Variegata' is a vigorous grower with narrow pale yellow margins to the leaves

practical project *1*

'SPRING CHORUS'

YOU WILL NEED

A piece of driftwood
An oval wooden board
A screw
A base, covered in green fabric

BETTER FOLIAGE
My favourite companion for daffodils is Pittosporum tenuifolium *and the white-tipped foliage of the variety 'Garnettii'. If you give away a bunch of daffodils, add a spray or two of pittosporum. It looks much better than the daffodil leaves – these are best not picked but left to die naturally to replenish the bulb for next year.*

There is nothing like the thrill of picking the first daffodils from your own garden. Daffodils are not the easiest flowers to arrange. They grow in groups, facing outwards and this is, naturally, the way they look best. Their stems do not lend themselves to graceful curves and the leaves are floppy and don't penetrate the foam readily, but, after a winter starved of garden flowers, it is joy to arrange them.

Often naturalised in the wild, daffodils look superb arranged with driftwood. A piece of scrubbed tree root has been used as a background in this loose, asymmetrical triangle arrangement. It is fixed permanently to an oval wooden board, 1cm (1/2in) deep and 30cm (12in) at the widest part. A screw is inserted from under the base of the board into the driftwood to make it stand (fig 1a). A second base, covered in green fabric, is added to give weight to the arrangement.

MATERIALS

The container
A green plastic oasis saucer

Foliage
Pittosporum tenuifolium
E.laeagnus maculata
Ivy *(Hedera helix* 'Gracilis')

Flowers:
Double daffodils

▪ Set up the driftwood with the saucer of oasis tucked close to it at the foot. Place it on a suitable base.
▪ Insert three branches of pittosporum of varying lengths, the tallest at the back, forming a loose asymmetrical triangle.
▪ Add shorter branches of elaeagnus, four or five, depending on how leafy they are. Place some to curve forwards and other still shorter ones to the back of the design (fig 1b).
▪ Add the daffodils, at varying heights. Don't place them all facing forwards, although the stems should look as if they grow from one central point.
▪ Finally, add a few sprigs of ivy at the base to conceal the dish and trail to the sides of the display. A final touch is to perch a small robin on the branch.

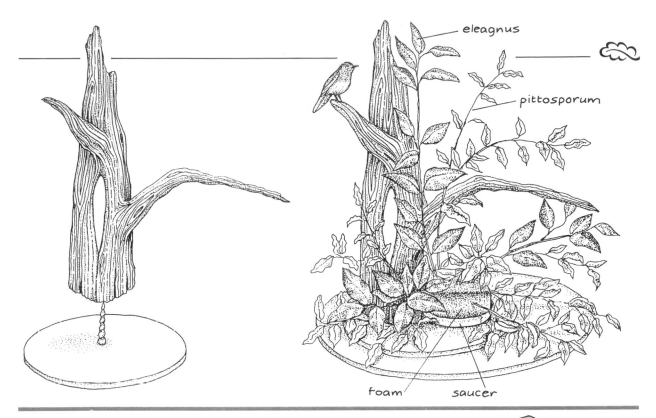

eleagnus

pittosporum

foam   saucer

These branches of viburnum were first conditioned with boiling water (see page 137) and forced into early flower in a low dish above a fireplace. Although they do not last long, they are a delight in the grey days of late winter.

MATERIALS

The container
A pewter entree dish. The steel grey colour is a perfect foil to the pinks of the blossom

Foliage
Cardoon *(Cynara cardunculus)*
Convolvulus cneorum

Flowers
Viburnum bodnantense 'Dawn'

- Press a little oasis fix to the base of the frog and position on the dish, slightly off centre to the left. Impale the soaked oasis on top.
- Insert the conditioned sprays of viburnum blossom first, to give a curving outline with shorter sprigs at the base (fig 2a).
- Add four to five grey cardoon leaves to the back and sides, and one curving over the lip of the container to the front.
- Add sprigs of grey convolvulus to fill in at the base (fig 2b). Top up the container with water.

practical
project
2

'RENEWAL'

(see picture, page 19)

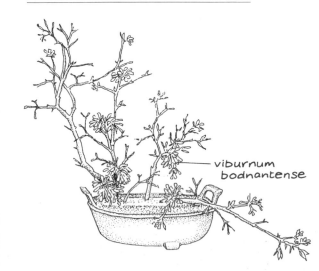

viburnum
bodnantense

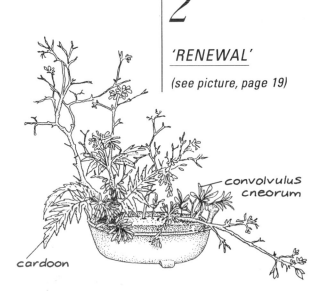

convolvulus
cneorum

cardoon

MARCH

This hopeful month can be a very satisfying and rewarding one yet
it can sometimes be very disappointing. Just like the birds we
experience an urge to 'get out and get on' in the garden, and then
the weather can dampen all our expectations. It should be the
month when we sow, transplant, take cuttings, dig in easily
worked soil and, on good days, get out the sun loungers and make
plans in the sunshine. It seems that weather patterns change, and
in recent years this month has been predominantly wet and windy
in most parts of the country. Was it always that way? Is it just a
childhood memory of fluffy lambs and primroses?

It is an exciting month none the less. The pruning of the roses is
one of the major tasks this month. It transforms the garden to see
the newly pruned roses in revitalised soil, and there is a tangible
feeling of expectancy. Flower arranging is easy with delightful
spring bulbs and the incredible little hacquetia – if you don't know
this 'green flower' with its yellow button centre and ruff of green
bracts, find a friend who has it, as it is best divided in early spring!

Two other invaluable flower-arranging plants – hostas and
bergenia – can be bought and planted or propagated by division
this month also, and will provide plenty of large leaves for the
centre of a flower arrangement in their first year. Other plants are
on the increase – the seedlings sown the previous month will be
growing encouragingly and some time later in the month need to be
pricked out into larger trays or pots to give them more room to
develop. Greenhouses get to the satisfying crowded stage and for
those without one, every spare inch of space on windowsills and
conservatories is in use. This month may often be cold, but the
whole of the flower-arranging year and a gardening summer is
ahead of us. It is a good month.

tasks

FOR THE

month

PICKING AND PRUNING
Picking roses for flower arranging
also prunes the bush during the
summer, and removing dead
flower heads regularly
encourages continued flowering.
Cut off the flower stems to a
strongly growing bud.

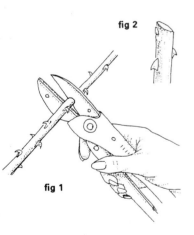

fig 2

fig 1

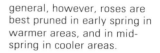

CHECKLIST

- ☐ Prick out and transplant half-hardy annuals sown last month
- ☐ Prune roses now unless you have pruned them in the autumn
- ☐ Take softwood cuttings of herbaceous perennials
- ☐ Start dahlia tubers into growth (see p38)

MAINTENANCE

HALF-HARDY ANNUALS

Half-hardy annuals planted last month will be ready for transplanting into new compost to give them more space and fresh nutrients to encourage consistent growth. You will need additional seed trays filled with a compost specially formulated for seedlings. If germination has been good you may need to discard some seedlings, but pot up as many as you can. You can always give them away when they reach a decent size.

Pricking out

Most of the seed planted towards the end of last month will by now show two sturdy leaves.

- Fill the trays and level as before. Make rows of evenly spaced holes with a pencil or dibber, 3–5cm (1½–2in) apart.
- Lift the seedlings by their leaves, easing them out with a spatula or plant label, easing them gently into their new holes and firming them with the spatula.
- Grow the seedlings on, if possible in the same temperature in which they germinated. Unfortunately many of us have to move them from a sunny window sill to an unheated

greenhouse – or move out of the house ourselves to make room for them!
- Don't overwater them to begin with as seedlings are prone to damping off.

PRUNING ROSES

The best time of year to prune roses is as open to debate as the origins of the rose. If you grow your roses where there is little risk of heavy frost affecting them, you will get the best results by pruning them at the end of the summer. Despite the cold, coastal climate in my garden, I invariably prune mine in late autumn, in order to get as long a period of flowering as possible. There are two main 'flushes'. If I prune in early spring, the first flush is later and only in a good summer will there be two. So there are exceptions to the general rule. In

general, however, roses are best pruned in early spring in warmer areas, and in mid-spring in cooler areas.

How to prune

- Use sharp secateurs to give a precise, clean cut.
- Choose a dormant, *outward facing* bud.
- Slope each cut backwards, from about 6mm (¼in) above the bud to a point on the opposite side of the stem that is about level with the top of the bud (fig 1). The cut is made on a slant so that rain will run off and help prevent disease (fig 2).
- Cut out damaged, dead and diseased wood, easily recognisable by its brown cross section. Healthy wood is creamy in colour.
- Cut out crossing stems and those growing inwards, to open up the centre of the bush. Cut off weak spindly growth, either to the main stem or leaving only a bud or two to restrict the amount of growth they have to maintain (fig 3).

How much to prune
Newly planted roses –
These are treated slightly differently from pruning in subsequent years. Prune hard to dormant buds about 15cm (6in) above ground level. This hard pruning encourages the root system to become established before

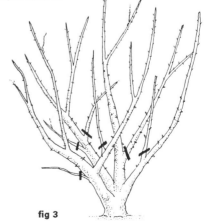

fig 3

the new shoots appear from the base.

Established roses:
Hybrid teas (large-flowered). Cut away about one third of the length of the new green shoots of the previous year's growth. For flower arranging, it is often a good idea to cut one stem only, very severely, as for a newly planted rose. This encourages vigorous growth from the base and long stems. Hard pruning produces better and bigger blooms but fewer of them (fig 4).

Floribundas (cluster-flowered). These are pruned less severely, new shoots to about one third of their length and dark wood to about half (fig 5).

Climbers. Don't follow the rule for new roses. Climbers should *not* be cut back too hard, but should be pruned so that they will grow into the shape you want. Cut away any damaged stems to a bud which is facing the way you want a branch to grow. Cut out completely any branches coming forwards in a direction that you do *not* want, for example, over a path, again cutting to a bud that will grow in the direction you want to train it.

Once the rose is established, the flowering heads should always be cut back to a bud as soon as they have finished flowering. In the autumn, follow the general pruning rules as above, cutting the leaders back to strong new growth and the strongest flowering side shoots to about half their length. Cut out completely any old stems that no longer produce new side shoots.

Ramblers: such as 'Albertine'. These are pruned immediately after they have finished flowering. Cut flower-bearing stems to almost ground level. Strong

new stems will appear over the summer and should be tied in to form a framework for the following year. *Shrub roses* such as 'Nevada'. These need very little pruning except to keep them within bounds.

The classification includes many of the old roses which, if you have room for them, are the most beautiful and interesting of all. *Species roses* such as *Rosa glauca* (syn. *R. rubrifolia*). These are what most of us think of as wild roses and are, in fact, shrubs. Like the shrub roses they need little pruning, but since many of these are useful to the flower arranger for their foliage, prune some shoots down to the base to produce new long growths.

PROPAGATION

SOFTWOOD CUTTINGS

Softwood cuttings are taken early in the year and, as the name implies, they are taken from shoots that are still soft. This is a suitable method of propagation for geraniums, pelargoniums, fuchsias and herbaceous perennials. Taken in the same way as semi-ripe and hardwood cuttings (see page 86) softwood cuttings at this time of year need heat and protection to root. As the cuttings are soft and sappy they lose moisture quickly. They root best in a close, constantly damp atmosphere, which is not so easy for the beginner to provide. If you have a heated greenhouse or can provide bottom heat with soil warming cables in a cold greenhouse, this gives them an ideal start. Failing that a simple electrically heated propagator is the next best thing. It provides bottom heat, with a heating element (10–12 watt) in the base and usually a ventilation shutter in the

lid. The seed tray or pots are placed inside it. Larger and more expensive propagators (up to 65 watt) are thermostatically controlled. These take several seed trays and the temperature can be regulated to the exact level given on the seed packet. Germination is that much more efficient as a result.

Yet, even under more makeshift conditions, softwood cuttings *will* root. A seed tray with a clear plastic lid can act as an unheated propagator. Although the temperature is dependent on the surroundings, it provides a humid environment. Failing that, the base of a clear lemonade bottle, cut to fit over a plant pot, provides a mini-propagator (fig 6).

Taking softwood cuttings
■ Fill a pot with moist compost for cuttings, or a mixture of moist peat and coarse sand.

■ Take the cutting from recent growth while the stem is soft. Do not take cuttings from stems that are wilting.

■ Cut cleanly with a knife, below a node or leaf joint, taking a cutting 7.5–10cm (3–4in) long.

■ Remove the lower leaves and dip the end into hormone rooting powder, made especially for softwood cuttings. Shake off the excess powder by tapping the cutting lightly (excess rooting powder can be detrimental).

■ Using a dibber, make a hole in the compost and insert the cutting. Firm gently.

■ Water lightly. Provide cover in one of the ways described above.

■ Once the cuttings have rooted and an adequate root system has formed, remove them carefully and pot up into 9cm (3½in) pots.

fig 4

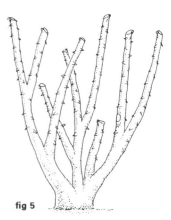
fig 5

fig 6

plants
OF THE
month

SKIMMIA
Skimmia reevesiana

Although a slow-growing shrub, it is very useful to the flower arranger. Its sturdy, glossy foliage is a good standby throughout the year. It combines particularly well with seasonal greenery, red carnations and with lilies whose own foliage should not be cut.

type	Evergreen, bushy shrub. Glossy leaves smell of oranges when crushed
flowers	Tiny clusters of star-like, fragrant, white flowers in early to mid-spring, scarlet berries in autumn
foliage	Rich green, oval, glossy. Very useful for giving depth to the centre of an arrangement
height	1.2m (4ft)
planting	In autumn or spring
position	Shade or semi-shade
soil	Fertile, moist soil
care	Too much sun or poor soil will cause yellowing of the leaves (chlorosis). Protect from frost
propagation	By semi-ripe cuttings with a heel in mid- and late summer
varieties for flower arranging	*S. japonica* 'Fructu-albo' has small, round, white berries (female)

HACQUETIA
Hacquetia epipactis

A delightful early spring-flowering plant, it looks like a green flower but has in fact an open face of five light green bracts with frilly edges with a small yellow dome in the centre. It grows in rounded clumps.

type	Deciduous, rhizomatous alpine
flowers	Tiny, yellow, buttons surrounded by a ruff of lime-green bracts on leafless stems from early to late spring
foliage	Trifoliate, bright green, with frilled edges
height	15cm (6in)
planting	In autumn
position	Light shade. Loses its lime-green colouring in full sun
soil	Well-drained, fertile soil
care	Keep roots cool. Grows well beside paving slabs or shady path
propagation	By division after flowering in late spring

CUSHION SPURGE
Euphorbia polychroma

A satisfying and startling mat of chrome-yellow flowers that appear rapidly in spring. The colour is at its best in spring, fading to a duller green by midsummer.

type	Deciduous perennial
flowers	Bright yellow bracts surrounding small flowers in mid- and late spring
foliage	Ovate, bright green, turning bronze green in autumn
height	38cm (15in)
planting	In autumn or early spring
position	Full sun
soil	Light, sandy soil gives best colour
care	Cut to ground level in autumn
propagation	By division
varieties for flower arranging	Annual varieties are well worth growing – *E.* 'Summer Icicle' has leaves and bracts veined and edged in white; *E. palustris* 'Magic Flute' has clusters of dainty, bright lime-green flower heads with cup-shaped bracts

BACHELOR'S BUTTONS
Kerria japonica 'Pleniflora'

This is a graceful shrub producing arching sprays of fluffy, golden, ball-shaped flowers. A perfect companion for narcissi. The small, serrated leaves on green stems are useful foliage for arrangements for the rest of the summer.

type	Deciduous shrub
flowers	Orange-yellow, double, with rounded heads in mid- and late spring
foliage	Bright green, ovate, sharply toothed leaves, carried on slender glossy green branches
height	3m (10ft)
planting	Mid-autumn to early spring
position	Sun or semi-shade, preferably against a wall
soil	Ordinary garden soil
care	Cut back all flowered shoots to strong new growths
propagation	By softwood cuttings in summer

practical
project
1

'SPRING GREEN'

The fresh green spring colours, with us for only a few weeks, are breathtaking after the drab days of winter. The succulent green of new beech leaves looks wonderful in an arrangement, but it must be properly conditioned to make it last (see pages 137-138).

This combination of the delicate lemon of the erythroniums, the vivid green of hacquetia and the unbelievable sulphur yellow of *Euphorbia polychroma* paints a portrait of spring. Sprigs of the vivid yellow rockery *Alyssum saxatile* were added to emphasise the lime-greens.

YOU WILL NEED

oasis

oasis tape

MATERIALS

The container
A tiered flower holder with four shallow cups that can take candles or flowers, or both, in the same cup

Foliage
Beech (Fagus), Choisya ternata 'Sundance' Euphorbia polychroma

Flowers
Narcissus 'Cheerfulness', Alyssum saxatile Erythronium, Hacquetia epipactis Spirea arguta

CANDLE CUPS
To adapt a candlestick to hold flowers, you will need a candle 'cup' from a florist, sold especially for this purpose. They are made in metal or plastic and come in several sizes. They have a narrow neck below a cup-shaped bowl which fits into the top of the candlestick. The oasis foam is taped into the cup and the tape taken around oasis, bowl and the bottleneck to make it firm. Lamp bases can also be adapted to hold flowers this way.

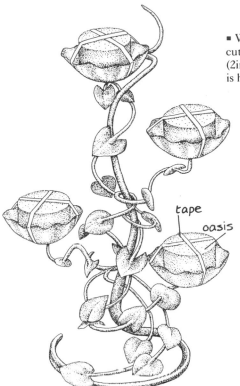

tape

oasis

■ Wedge a round of soaked oasis into each cup, cutting it to size so that the foam is about 5cm (2in) above the lip of the cup. Tape it so that it is held firmly (fig 1a).

■ Insert a spray of beech in the top cup to establish the height of the display and shorter sprays of beech to make a roughly triangular outline in each cup. Keep the foliage in the lower units short so that each is fairly separate, with just the trailing ends of foliage merging.

■ Add very short sprigs of choisya to make the background for the delicate flowers and to cover the oasis, as in the bottom left hand cup (fig 1b).

■ Add short stems of narcissi, heads of euphorbia and sprigs of golden alyssum and begin to fill each unit.

■ Finally add stems as long as possible of erythronium and hacquetia throughout with a few short trails of white *Spirea arguta* (fig 1c).

NOTE

■ *Any raised container, like this one, gives a lightness to flowers and foliage as the space around each group becomes part of the design. A branched candlestick can easily be adapted to hold flowers and give a similar effect by the addition of candle cups. A group of single candlesticks of varying heights with cups will create an equally stunning effect* ■

Beech

narcissi

choisya

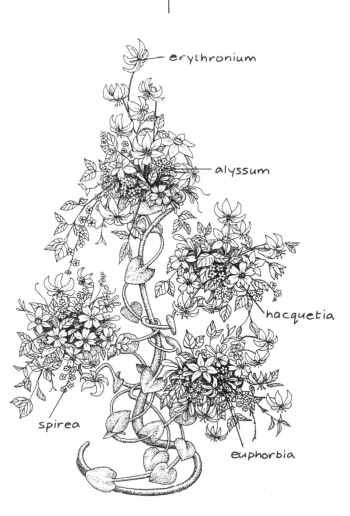

erythronium

alyssum

hacquetia

spirea

euphorbia

practical
project
2

'GLEAMS IN THE
GLOAMING'

YOU WILL NEED

a large block of oasis foam
chicken wire
florist's tape

The russet colours of autumn are a surprise in springtime, but the new spring growth of *Spiraea japonica* 'Gold Flame' is in just those delightful colours. The gold, russet red and sepia shades blend happily with the subdued tones of the comfortable library, where a strident display of brightly coloured flowers would detract from the timeless feeling of leisure and repose.

MATERIALS

The container
A large copper jug

Foliage
Spiraea japonica 'Gold Flame'
Skimmia reevesiana 'Rubella'

Flowers
Bachelor's buttons (*Kerria japonica* 'Pleniflora')
Narcissi

■ Wedge the block of oasis in the neck of the jug so that it stands about 8cm (3in) above the lip. Crumple the chicken wire to fit loosely around the foam and use tape to hold it firm (fig 2a).

■ Establish the height and width of the arrangement with an outline of spiraea. The height of the tallest branch should not be more than one and half times the height of the jug.
■ Create a loose, 'all round' outline with spirea. Then fill in the centre with shorter sprays of the dark green, glossy skimmia by way of contrast.
■ Keeping inside the outline, add long sprays of kerria, allowing some to curve downwards over the lip of the jug (fig 2b).
■ When you are satisfied with the outline and it looks good from all sides, add the narcissi at different heights, facing in different directions.

NOTE

■ *Jugs make ideal holders for a casual arrangement, when you want to create a natural and uncontrived effect. You will need to adapt the jug to take the foliage. If you just stick it straight into a jug of water, it will not take many stems, and they will be held stiffly upright without the lavishness and looseness of this display* ■

APRIL

This month is one of the highlights of the gardening year. The
spring garden is an immensely satisfying one – rockeries look like
Persian carpets; woodlands and flower beds are awash with the
whites and yellows of narcissi and erythroniums; the blue of the
smaller bluebells and grape hyacinths looks delightful under trees
thick with pink and white blossom. Even the blue of the sky seems
more vivid after the overcast and stormy days of the previous
month. Showers there are, but not the searing cold rain that early
spring will sometimes throw at us. The weather now is altogether
softer and we can look forward to ever warmer days.

Real work can be done in the garden, with autumn-flowering
bulbs to plant and dahlias to bring into growth under glass or
inside the house. And as the soil warms up, the summer annuals
can be sown direct into the ground. There is still a risk of frost at
nights, even in late spring in some areas, so tender plants must
still be protected.

At this time of year the birds are just as busy in the garden as we
are, shyly fluttering off as we approach and returning to their
chosen spot when we leave them in peace. They contribute much to
the feeling of ease in a garden and, if we have fed them through the
barren days of winter, they remain loyal and bring added interest
with their activity.

Flower arranging now is a joy. Branches of blossom in big pots
need very little arranging, and even a single bloom of the camellia
is a feast for the eyes. We have the whole summer to look forward
to and lazy tea breaks in the sun are once again very much a part
of the pleasure of being in the garden.

tasks
FOR THE
month

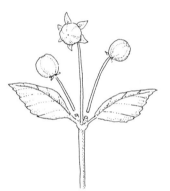

Stopping dahlias

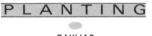

C H E C K L I S T

- Start dahlias into growth, divide or take cuttings
- Plant nerines
- Choose and plant lilies
- Choose and plant gladioli
- Sow hardy annuals outdoors

PLANTING

DAHLIAS

Although as a cut flower dahlias last well in water, they are not one of my favourites for a flower arrangement. Their stems are too stiff and the heads held forward so close to the stem that it is difficult to make them face in different directions. They sometimes don't seem to blend with other flowers, but instead can dominate a mixed display. They *are,* however, a spectacular and useful flower in their own right, and many flower arrangers are very fond of them.

Dahlias are tuberous-rooted, tender perennials. There are so many varieties, it is difficult to make a selection for flower arranging. In general, the open faces of the collerette varieties are the most useful, followed by the semi-cactus and decorative varieties.

In very sheltered and frost-free corners of the garden, plump dahlia tubers can be planted into well-cultivated ground at the end of this month, about 10cm (4in) below the surface of the soil, with a handful of bonemeal sprinkled into the planting hole. In colder areas, they can be started into growth under cover in order to get earlier blooms.

Starting dahlia tubers into growth

Place dahlias, stalk upwards, in a deep box. Spray them with tepid water and cover with damp peat. Keep them lightly moist in a cool greenhouse or indoors. The eyes on the crowns of the tubers will begin to swell. If they are fairly young tubers and you do not wish to propagate them, plant them out when they are growing strongly and when all danger of frost has passed.

PROPAGATION

DIVIDING DAHLIAS

The new shoots arise from these crowns at the top of the clump of tuberous roots. The swollen root tubers themselves do not bear buds. The clump can be divided every few years, either in its dormant state or after starting them into growth this way and before planting out. It is easier to do the latter as each portion must have a piece of crown with at least one bud or new shoots and at least one tuber. The clumps are easy to split, using a knife. Dust the cut parts with flowers of sulphur to help prevent fungus. Plant the sections when there is no danger of frost, the following month in most areas. Plant in full sun, adding a handful of bonemeal to each planting hole.

Taking dahlia cuttings

This is a good way to increase stock from old tubers. Start them into

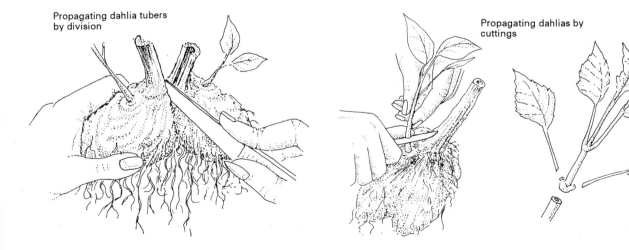

Propagating dahlia tubers by division

Propagating dahlias by cuttings

growth as above. When the shoots are about 5cm (2in) long, cut them off at the base with a sharp knife. Remove the lower leaves and cut the stem just below a joint. Dip into hormone rooting powder and insert into cuttings compost in boxes or pots. Treat them as for softwood cuttings (page 29), keeping them in a humid atmosphere until they have rooted.

Stopping dahlias

When dahlias are growing strongly, with several new flowering shoots, pinch out the tip of the main stem to encourage bushy growth.

PLANTING

NERINES

To grow some nerines you will need a heated greenhouse. There is, however, one variety, *N. bowdenii* (Guernsey lily) that is frost-hardy and can be grown anywhere. Under the best conditions, it will multiply rapidly.
Nerines have a peculiar habit of flowering – the rather fierce pink heads are produced in umbels at the end of long straight, leafless stems, about 50cm (2ft) high. The strap-shaped leaves appear just as the flowers are finished. They remain during the summer and die down over the winter. (For varieties see page 99.)

Planting nerines

- Nerines are sold both in spring and in autumn. Plant as soon as you receive the bulbs.
- Choose a sunny, sheltered border under a wall, so that they can benefit from the warmth of the wall.
- Prepare the planting holes in ordinary, well-drained soil and sprinkle a handful of bonemeal in the base of

each. Set the bulbs 5-8cm (2-3in) deep.
- Top-dress annually with leaf mould or well-rotted manure.
- Take care to allow the warmth of the sun to get at the bulbs during the summer and do not allow them to be shaded by dense foliage.

LILIES

Lilies are one of the most spectacular plants for formal flower arranging. When my only experience of them was stately florist's lilies, they were not one of my personal favourites. They seemed rather stiff, supercilious flowers. Once I started to grow them in my own garden I realised that some lilies give quite the wrong impression. They are not the difficult and demanding flowers they might seem, and my sandy garden soil with its good drainage and copious supplies of cow manure is, in fact, ideal.
Lilies are magnificent. I still regard them with something akin to awe when they are in bloom and wouldn't combine them with common garden annuals! As lilies like to grow with their roots in the shade and their heads in sun, they thrive in groups, in a bed of evergreen and deciduous shrubs.
Lilies are grouped as species, varieties and hybrids. The hybrids are classified into nine divisions to establish some order out of the profusion of lily types. The majority of lilies are hardy bulbs, summer-flowering and dormant in winter. The Madonna lily (*Lilium candidum*) is an exception that stands apart from the rest, both in its beauty and its requirements. It produces leaves in winter but flowers in summer. It also thrives in full sun and is planted in autumn.

It is impossible to underestimate the value of the lily to the flower arranger. In shape alone, the flower heads offer an amazing variety of forms. The trumpet lily is the most stately and the one which comes to mind when most people think of a lily, but lilies can be cup-shaped and pendulous, bowl-shaped and upright, star-shaped or, in the case of the Turk's cap lily, delicately reflexed. The lily is probably the most useful flower in the garden. (See p.82 for lilies to grow.)

Planting lilies

- Some lilies produce roots from the stem (that part of it which is underground) as well as from the base. These are known as stem-rooting lilies. Others produce roots only from the base and are known as basal rooting lilies. It is important to differentiate between them. Stem-rooting lilies must be planted more deeply, to provide their roots with water and nutrients, than those which grow only from the basal plate (the Madonna lily, the North American species and Bellingham hybrids).
- The soil should be fertile and well-manured, (lily specialist firms recommend cow manure), moist, with good drainage. Work the soil to a depth of 20cm (8in), incorporating compost and well-rotted manure. On heavy soils add a 5cm (2in) or so layer of sand at the base of the planting hole. If you cannot provide the right conditions for growth, grow lilies in large tubs instead.
- Plant stem-rooting lilies deeply, about 10–15cm (4–6in) below the soil, depending on the size of bulb.
- Plant basal rooting lilies about 5cm (2in) below the surface of the soil.
(continued on page 42)

turk's cap

bowl

star

cup

open trumpet

trumpet

plants
OF THE
month

RHODODENDRON
Rhododendron thomsonii

This species rhododendron makes a dominant and eye-catching shrub in a mixed border with its waxy, dark green leaves and peeling bark. It has startling red clusters of tubular flowers in spring.

type	Evergreen shrub
flowers	Clusters of bell-shaped, deep red flowers with a waxy texture, in spring
foliage	Shiny dark green with blue-grey undersides, useful in arrangements all year round
height	Up to 2.5m (8ft)
planting	Autumn
position	Sheltered, light woodland is ideal
soil	Sandy, well-drained loam. Will not tolerate lime
care	Mulch with leaf mould, manure or peat, to prevent the roots drying out
propagation	By layering or semi-hardwood cuttings
varieties for flower arranging	*R. williamsianum* has bell-shaped, soft pink flowers with very attractive bronze foliage when young

WARMINSTER BROOM
Cytisus × praecox

Brooms are valuable for flower arranging to give sweeping curves or a graceful outline. The stems are pliable and can be gently eased to the desired shape. The flowers are not significant for flower displays.

type	Deciduous, densely branched, arching shrub
flowers	Cascades of creamy yellow pea-like flowers in mid- to late spring
foliage	Arching branches with tiny ovate grey-green leaves, each with three leaflets that appear after the flowers. Invaluable for arranging
height	1.5m (60in)
planting	In autumn or spring
position	Full sun
soil	Poor to ordinary, well-drained soil
care	Often short-lived. Needs replacing every 4–5 years when it looks woody and ceases to flower
propagation	From seed in spring or by heel cuttings in late summer
varieties for flower arranging	*C. × p.* 'Allgold' has bright yellow flowers; *C. × kewensis* is procumbent and spreading

VIBURNUM
Viburnum tinus

Wonderful varieties of both deciduous and evergreen viburnum mean that this shrub is available to the flower arranger all the year round. In mid-winter the evergreen *V. tinus* is invaluable both for its foliage and the constant supply of dainty flower clusters.

type	Evergreen, hardy shrub
flowers	Pink buds opening to white in flat heads, 5–7.5cm (2–3in) across, late autumn to mid-spring
foliage	Oval, dark green leaves
height	Up to 3m (10ft)
planting	In spring or autumn
position	Full sun, sheltered from cold winds that could curl and brown the tips of the leaves
soil	Well-drained, fertile soil
care	Cut the lowest sweeping branches for flower arranging to keep the shrub tidy
propagation	Semi-hardwood cuttings in autumn
varieties for flower arranging	*V. tinus* 'Eve Price' has pink flowers

ROBB'S SPURGE
Euphorbia robbiae

One of the most attractive euphorbias – and all of them have some value for flower arranging. The stems should be charred when cut as the milky latex exuded by the stem is an irritant.

type	Evergreen perennial
flowers	Small, insignificant with conspicuous disc-like bracts in limey-yellow, forming spikes
foliage	Dull, leathery, dark green, obovate leaves
height	30–45cm (12–18in)
planting	In autumn to spring
position	Prefers shade
soil	Tolerant of most soils
care	Remove flowering stems to encourage new shoots
propagation	By seed in early spring or by division in autumn
varieties for flower arranging	*E. palustris* is a bushy perennial with sulphur-yellow bracts; cushion spurge *(E. epithymoides)* is a rounded, bushy perennial with green leaves and heads of bright yellow bracts

tasks

FOR THE

month

'NANUS' GLADIOLI FOR FLOWER ARRANGING

Bulb catalogues often have a mixed selection on offer which make a pretty group under the shelter of a wall.

'The Bride' (bridal gladioli) – creamy white, very pale lime-green marking inside the petals

'Prince Claus' – white, with pinkish red marking inside

'Guernsey Glory' – pink with red markings outlining a cream blotch on the throat and red stamens.

'Good Luck' – delightful peachy, salmon shade, red markings inside.

'Impressive' – soft pink, with strong crimson markings

GLADIOLUS

Gladioli, or Sword lilies, are half-hardy, cormous plants and there are several quite distinct types. The hybrids are divided into:
Grandiflorus or *Large-flowered* – robust plants of up to 1.2m (48in) with flower spikes of 50cm (2ft) between midsummer and early autumn;
Butterfly – smaller than large-flowered types, less robust, dense spikes of flowers, 45cm (18in) long, often blotched in deeper shades on the throat, flowering in mid- and late summer, strident colours;
Primulinus – hooded flowers, loosely arranged, free-flowering spikes 38cm (15in) mid- to late summer, prettier colour range than the two above;
Miniature – florets are similar to the primulinus types but smaller, on 38cm (15in) long flower spikes.

Large-flowered gladioli – have one-sided spikes of large flowers set closely together on strong stems. These are readily available from a florist and, unless you are decorating a

church or making a very large display, they can look stiff and ungainly in a flower arrangement. They are not really worth giving space in a small garden, as they are so readily available in the shops.

'Nanus' gladioli hybrids are a different matter. These belong to the miniature group and are perfect for flower arranging. They have small, delicate flowers on slender stems reaching about 45–60cm (18–24in) and flower in early to midsummer. They also throw up secondary spikes, which makes them perfect for flower arranging.

Corms can be planted in spring or autumn (see page 109). If planted now in a frost free situation, they will survive cold winters and can be left in the ground permanently.

PROPAGATION

SOWING HARDY ANNUALS OUTDOORS

Hardy annuals can stand some frost and so can be sown either in the autumn for overwintering in light,

free-draining soil, as with sweet peas (see page 96), or directly in the open ground in early spring, once the ground has warmed up. There is little point, however, in sowing hardy annuals too early in the year or in cold wet ground – the seed will lie dormant and may rot. Annuals can fill in gaps in a border with a riot of colour. Alternatively, you may want to plant a bed consisting only of annuals, according to a special colour scheme, and perhaps include some half-hardy annuals in late spring. In this case, outline the areas to be sown with annuals either with canes, or trickle sand or perlite around the allotted spaces. Within these shapes, sow the seed in rows. It is much easier to recognise an annual from a weed when seed is sown in rows.

Getting the best results
- Choose a sunny spot in the garden with well-drained, not-too-rich soil.
- Fork over the ground, break up any lumps and tread it lightly. Rake over the surface of the soil to get a fine tilth.
- Outline the shape of each area to be sown.

back of border

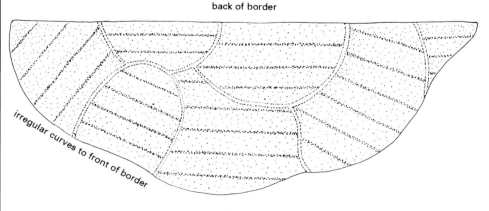

irregular curves to front of border

sow in straight lines within each shape

• Use the back of a hoe to make straight rows of drills, 1cm (½in) deep and 15cm (6in) apart for low-growing plants and 30cm (12in or more) apart for taller plants.

• Tip the seeds into the palm of your hand, mix very small seeds with white sand for easier sowing. Sprinkle the seeds along the lines of the drills as thinly as possible to minimise the amount of thinning later. Sow from the back of the border to the front to avoid trampling a sown area.
• Gently push the soil over the seed with the back of the rake.
• Water gently but thoroughly, using a fine rose on a watering can.

Aftercare
Do not allow the soil to dry out. Hand-weed carefully between the rows. When the seedlings germinate, they will still be too close together, despite careful sowing. Competing for light and plant nutrients hinders their development and, if they are not thinned out, they will become long and spindly with thin weak stems. When the seedlings are large enough to handle, pull out the weakest, leaving about twice as many as you will eventually want. Leave about 2.5cm (1in) between them. After a few weeks, when they are sturdy seedlings, thin out a second time to about 15cm (6in) apart. Stake taller growing plants early with twigs to encourage straight stems for flower arranging (see page 63).

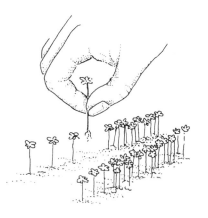

first thinning

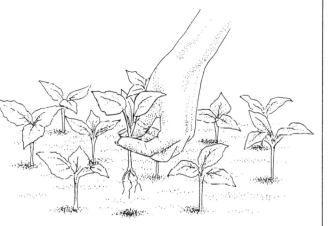

second thinning

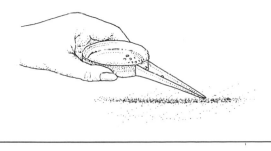

HAND HELD SEED DISPENSER

• *Working outdoors with fine seeds on a windy day can be tricky. Small gadgets such as a hand-held seed sower give better spacing of seed sown indoors and are a boon for sowing direct into the open ground* ■

HARDY ANNUALS FOR FLOWER ARRANGING

Baby's breath *(Gypsophila)*
Californian poppy *(Eschscholzia)*
Candytuft *(Iberis)*
Sweet basil *(Ocimum)* – grow for foliage
Carthamus – an everlasting
Chrysanthemum – annual
Clarkia elegans
Clary *(Salvia horminium)*
China aster *(Callistephus)*
Cornflower *(Centaurea)*
Euphorbia 'Summer Icicle'
Flax *(Linum)*
Godetia
Hawksbeard *(Crepis)*
Larkspur (annual delphinium)
Love-in-a-mist *(Nigella)*
Malva *(Malope)*
Annual mallow *(Lavatera)*
Marigold *(Calendula)*
Poppy *(Papaver)*
Prickly poppy *(Argemone)*
Scabious *(Scabiosa)*
Shoo-fly plant *(Nicandra)* – berries dry well
Tidy tips *(Layia)*
Woodruff *(Asperula)* – fragrant
Zinnia 'Envy'

practical
project
1

'BLOSSOM TIME'

The Viridiflora tulip is one of the most exciting flowers to arrange. The many shades in the different varieties allow many combinations with the spring foliages. The tufted delicacy of new larch is a perfect foil for the strong markings of the viridifloras, and the two make a simple and delightful combination on their own.

This is a more flamboyant display combining blossom and the large flowerheads of rhododendron making a particularly strong association.

MATERIALS

The container

A large shallow bowl, not seen, standing on a columnar plant pedestal. These pedestals make an interesting change, when used to hold a flower arrangement instead of plants.

Foliage
Broom *(Cytisus)*
Larch *(Larix)*

Flowers
Prunus blossom
Rhododendron thomsonii
Viridiflora tulip 'Spring Green'

YOU WILL NEED
a large block oasis
chicken wire
florist's tape

■ Cut the block of oasis in half and wedge the two pieces together, on end, in the bowl so that they project at least 5cm (2in) above the rim. Cover with scrumpled chicken wire and secure with tape (fig 1a). Place the bowl on the pedestal and work 'in situ'.

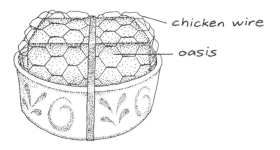

chicken wire

oasis

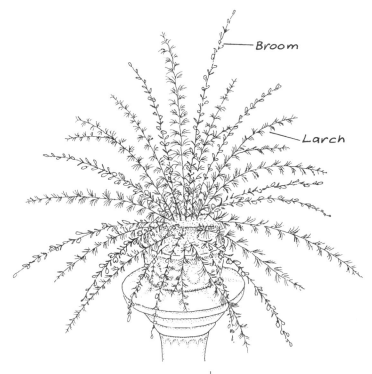

Broom

Larch

■ Curve the broom in arching branches and outline a roughly triangular shape. Add long branches of larch, sweeping downwards. Avoid making the sprays the same length on both sides as this will look too uniform (fig 1b).

■ Add the sprays of prunus blossom within this outline, with some coming forwards so that the arrangement does not look flat and one-dimensional.

■ Insert short branches of rhododendron to the centre of the display and finally add the tulips, cutting the stems to vary the lengths (fig 1c).

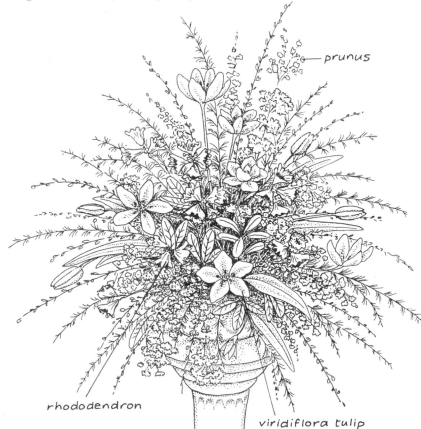

prunus

rhododendron

viridiflora tulip

NOTE

■ *New spring foliage – larch, broom and blossom – must all be properly conditioned by boiling the stem ends and then allowing them to stand in water for at least two hours (see page 137)* ■

FLEXIBLE BROOM
Broom is a very useful foliage for the flower arranger. It is very pliable and can be bent into graceful curves with the warmth of the hand. To bend it into sharp curves, tie it in circles of the size you want, soak for a few hours in tepid water and it will keep that curve when the ties are removed.

practical project
2
'STEEL SCULPTURE'

YOU WILL NEED

2 × 25cm (10in) candles
2 plastic candle holders for
floral foam
florist's tape
oasis

Camellias are aristocrats, with exquisite flowers, clean, sculptured lines and strong, glossy foliage. They really need no other companions. Display them on a low table where you can look down on to the faces of the flowers and the inside of the petals with their attractive stamens.

MATERIALS

The container
The container is a polished steel candle holder with cups for flowers or candles. Cut glass or crystal also look well with camellias. To convert a candlestick to hold flowers see page 32.

Flowers and foliage
Camellia japonica
'C. M. Wilson'

▪ Cut small blocks of oasis to fit the cups. Wrap with tape to hold them firmly.

▪ Insert the candle holders into the foam. Cut 2.5cm (1in) off the end of one candle to make them of different heights. Press a small piece of the sticky oasis-fix to the inside of each candle holder (this will hold the candles absolutely upright) and insert the candles into the higher block of oasis.

▪ Cut very short sprigs of foliage and arrange these around the outside of the foam, also adding single leaves to conceal the foam.

▪ Add camellia buds to the outside, open flowers against the candle bases and a solitary open flower head in the lower holder.

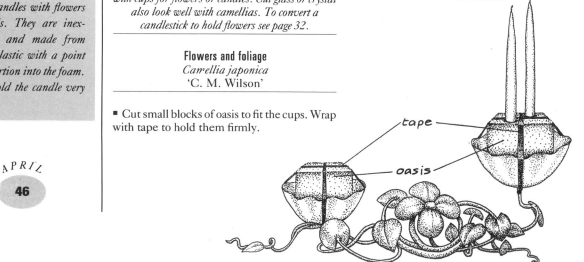

tape

oasis

plants
OF THE
month

CAMELLIA
Camellia japonica 'C. M. Wilson'

These popular and immensely attractive shrubs have everything – handsome foliage, perfectly formed blooms, single, semi-double and double flowers and soft colours. Even the reds are not strident. Given the right frost free conditions they are easy to grow.

type	Generally hardy, evergreen shrub
flowers	Light pink, anemone-form, outdoors early to mid-spring
foliage	Glossy, deep green, broadly ovate, leathery leaves. Lasts well in water
height	Up to 3m (10ft)
planting	In early to mid-autumn or spring
position	Light shade. Grows well against walls. Can be grown in large pots
soil	Well-drained, neutral to acid
care	Protect from morning frost and shelter from wind. Prune to shape after flowering
propagation	By semi-ripe or hardwood cuttings, in midsummer to autumn
varieties for flower arranging	*C. j.* 'Adolphe Audusson' has large, semi-double red flowers with yellow stamens; *C. williamsii* 'Donation' has large, semi-double pink flowers and is free flowering

VIRIDIFLORA TULIPS
Tulipa

Formal bedding schemes of uniform ranks of the stiff-stemmed Darwin tulips can make it seem rather a boring flower – yet, the Viridiflora tulip is, to me, one of the most exciting and impressive spring flowers around.

As the name implies, the flower head is splashed with green. There are numerous varieties in colour combinations, both curious and exotic. With some varieties the leaves are an ornament in themselves. You may need to buy them from a specialist bulb nursery, but they are well worth the trouble.

type	Deciduous bulb
flowers	Six-petalled, wide range of colours, each splashed with green
foliage	Lance-shaped; some varieties have spectacular white margins to the leaf, giving it a sculptured look
height	25–60cm (10–24in), depending on variety
planting	In early to late autumn
position	Sun to light shade
soil	Well fed, free-draining soil
care	Lift the bulbs and store them in a dry shed or garage. If left in the ground, pull off the leaves and stems once they have withered completely. Do not obscure the bulbs too much with other planting as they need the warmth of the sun to ripen. Feed in early spring with a high potash fertiliser
propagation	Divide bulbs from new bulblets and plant separately
varieties for flower arranging	'Spring Green' has ivory petals splashed with green; 'Esperanto' is rose with deep green marking on each petal and superb foliage, edged in silvery white; 'Artist' has a sculptured shape with twisted, pointed petals, shaded rose, purplish green, apricot; 'Golden Artist' has petals of same formation as 'Artist' but is a golden yellow flushed with apricot

MAY

This is the month of blossom and the exquisite limey-green of new leaf growth as the buds open. Choice shrubs and foliage plants like hostas and euphorbias produce shoots of incredible delicacy and colour. Later in the year, the sun drains the colour and some of the first vibrancy of the plant is lost. Although it is a joy to watch this new foliage unfold, much of it is of little use to the flower arranger until it has hardened off, later in the month. Soft hosta leaves wilt quickly when they are put in water and, apart from azaleas and rhododendrons, branches of blossom are short-lived indoors. Conditioning them well before use makes them last much longer. Now is also the time of year when differences in climate seem to be most marked. This tends to be quite a dry month everywhere and, since it is also a month of rapid growth in the garden as the soil warms up and plants respond to the rise in air temperature, it is often necessary to water the garden. This applies particularly to newly planted out half-hardy annuals and recently planted shrubs.

From the flower arranger's point of view, surprisingly, late spring can be a difficult time. The new foliage is very tempting, but it is soft and quite unreliable in water and so we are still stuck mainly with evergreens. Flowers are not yet plentiful in the garden either. It is an in-between season in most areas, except in those corners with a very favourable climate. Some bulbs are ready for lifting and we long for the perennials, annuals and roses.
It's also the month to think about the tubs and pots on the patio. They give great scope for taking the principles of flower arranging outside – experimenting with groups of containers, arranging shapes, colours and foliage together. Although they will require some attention for most of the year, this is the month to get the main backbone of the planting done.

tasks

FOR THE

month

**BIENNIALS FOR
FLOWER ARRANGING**

PLANTS TO BE SOWN NOW:
Canterbury bell *(Campanula)*
Cheiranthus
Double daisy *(Bellis)*
Forget-me-not *(Myosotis)*
Foxglove *(Digitalis)*
Honesty *(Lunaria)*
Hound's tongue *(Cynoglossum)*
Stock *(Matthiola)*
Sweet William *(Dianthus barbatus)*
Viola

CHECKLIST

- Harden off half-hardy annuals before planting in their permanent site
- Tie cordon-grown sweet peas into a support
- Sow hardy biennials
- Propagate lilac from tip cuttings (see p.58)
- Choose shrubs and foliage plants for arranging in containers

MAINTENANCE

This is the month to deal with some of the flower arranger's all-time favourites – sweet peas, lilies, carnations and pinks – and to harden off the half-hardy annuals for planting in the flower beds.

HARDENING OFF PLANTS

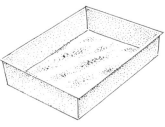

This is a gradual process after they have been protected or overwintered under cover. Their source of warmth must be removed by degrees, and they need to be exposed over a period of days to outdoor conditions to harden off the plant tissue. The ideal situation is where the plants start life in a heated greenhouse, the ventilation is gradually increased and they are then transferred to a cold frame. The frame is left open during the day and closed at night. After a few days and in suitable weather, the frame is left open at night also, to complete this hardening off process. It takes more effort but it is just as possible to harden off the plants with more makeshift arrangements, taking plants out during the day and bringing them back into a conservatory or porch at night. If you don't have a cold greenhouse or

conservatory, it is worth investing in a cold frame, making an improvised one from a wooden box or drawer with a lid of bubble polythene. Bubble polythene has good light diffusing properties as well as providing insulation.

Planting out half-hardy annuals
Once the plants have been hardened off gradually and after all danger of frost has passed, this is the month to plant them out in their permanent homes.
- Remove them from their pots or trays with as much root as possible. The easiest way is to ease out the whole trayful and tease or cut them apart with a knife.
- Lay the individual plants where they are to be planted, taking time to imagine how they will look in flower and group them accordingly.
- Use a trowel to make holes deep enough to accommodate all the root system and gently water the holes with the hose.
- Insert the plant and firm in gently with the hands.

SWEET PEAS

Sweet peas planted in late winter should be growing strongly and will have formed side shoots as a result of pinching out the tip from the first seed growth (see page 21). They can be hardened off and planted in their permanent positions. Sweet peas for flower arranging can be left to grow freely, but if you want to grow extra large blooms, say, for a wedding bouquet or even to exhibit, you will have to grow them as cordons, that is, restrict the growth to one main stem.

Cordon-grown sweet peas
- Select the strongest growing stem once the plants are about 25cm (10in)

high. Tie it loosely, with metal ring ties or twine, to a cane on to the trellis framework.

■ Snip off the remainder of the shoots using small scissors.

■ Continue to remove all the tendrils and side shoots as the plant grows, so that it will produce extra large blooms but only on the main stem.

PROPAGATION

SOWING HARDY BIENNIALS

Biennials are sown one year, flower and seed the next year, and so their life cycle is two years. To get the best flowering display, some herbaceous perennials are also best treated as biennials, for example wallflowers *(Cheiranthus)*.

Although biennials can be sown later, sowing now ensures they have become sturdy plants by autumn and withstand frosts. The main

difference between sowing biennials and annuals is that hardy annuals are sown and flower in the same place, while biennials are usually sown in boxes or in a nursery bed and transplanted later in the year, even as late as mid-autumn, to where they will eventually flower.

Sowing and transplanting

■ Prepare the seed bed as for hardy annuals (see pages 42–3).
■ If sown in boxes, transplant the seedlings when they are large enough to handle into the nursery bed, 15–20cm (6–8in) apart. Keep well watered and weed-free.
■ First make the holes where the plants are to go, using a hand trowel. Water the hole.
■ Using a small fork, lift the plant with a ball of soil to avoid disturbing the roots.
■ Place it in the prepared hole without crushing the root system and gently firm the soil around it.
■ As before, keep the plants watered and weed-free.

Forget-me-not and honesty self-seed very freely and usually appear each year without sowing new seed. So does columbine *(Aquilegia)*, but these are now also available in wonderful colour combinations for flower arranging and named varieties such as 'McKana Giants' so that it is more rewarding to sow new seed each year to flower the next. Columbine is poisonous.

Perennials that are sown each year like biennials are usually those used in spring bedding schemes, such as wallflowers *(Cheiranthus)*, when the ground is needed for annuals. Some are short-lived and better stock is obtained from new seed, such as double daisy *(Bellis perennis)*, clary *(Salvia)*, *Verbascum*, Sweet William *(Dianthus barbatus)*.

SHRUBS AND FOLIAGE PLANTS FOR CONTAINERS (see p.56)

Acer palmatum 'Dissectum Atropurpureum' – 1.5m (4ft)

Artemisia abrotanum (Southernwood) – 1m (3ft), semi-evergreen

Aucuba japonica – (Spotted laurel 'Variegata') – 1.5m (5ft)

Azalea – evergreen varieties, 60–75cm (2–2½ft), add extra peat

Berberis buxifolia 'Nana' – dark green leaves, good soil, 60cm (2ft)

Berberis thunbergii 'Aurea' dwarf type, bright yellow leaves, 60cm (2ft)

Buxus 'Latifolia maculata' compact shrub, yellow variegated, 1.8m (6ft)

Buxus sempervirens 'Elegantissima' – grey-green, silver edged leaves, 60cm (2ft)

Camellia 'Donation' – shelter from wind, flowers freely, 1.5m (5ft)

Cassiope lycopodioides – prostrate, spreading, add extra peat

Choisya ternata – aromatic glossy leaves, 1.8m (6ft)

Choisya ternata 'Sundance' – aromatic glossy leaves, 1.8m (6ft)

Cordyline australis (Cabbage palm) – sword-shaped leaves, to 1.8m (6ft)

Cytisus × *kewensis* (Broom) prostrate, trailing habit with yellow flowers

Daphne mezereum winter-flowering, best as a single specimen, 1.2m (4ft)

Elaeagnus pungens 'Maculata' – bright green and gold leaves, 1.5m (5ft)

Euonymus fortunei 'Emerald Gaiety' – prostrate gold-green leaves

Hebe albicans – rounded shrub, blue-grey leaves, white flowers, 60cm (2ft)

Helichrysum serotinum – silver-grey, tufted foliage, aromatic

Hydrangea macrophylla – many cultivars, best as single specimen, 1.2m (4ft)

Laurus nobilis – best as a specimen, glossy, dark green leaves, 1.5–2m (5–7ft)

Lavandula spica 'Hidcote' – compact plant, pale blue-grey flowers

Ligustrum ovalifolium 'Aureo-marginatum' (Golden privet) – keep this well pruned each autumn, wonderful yellow–midgreen leaf

Perovskia atriplicifolia 'Blue Spire' – greyish foliage, blue flowers, 90cm (3ft)

Phormium tenax 'Purpureum' and *P.t.* 'Variegatum' – 1.8m (6ft)

Ruta graveolens 'Jackman's Blue' – compact, blue-green leaves, 30cm (12in)

Senecio greyi – prune to shape and for new silver-grey leaves, 90cm (3ft)

Vinca minor (Lesser periwinkle) – trailing, dark leaves, blue flowers

Vinca minor 'Elegantissima' – less vigorous than above, variegated

The height is only approximate as any plant with its roots restrained in a container will not reach the height that it would in a border

plants

OF THE

month

LESSER PERIWINKLE
Vinca minor 'Alba Variegata'

This is a plant that you can keep in a tub so you always have trails of variegated dainty foliage for an arrangement. Any of the periwinkles are good, but the *Vinca major* – the most commonly grown – will run riot over anything else you plant with it. *Vinca major* 'Variegata' is less invasive.

type	Evergreen, ground cover sub-shrub
flowers	Tubular, white, 2.5cm (1in) across, in mid-spring to midsummer
foliage	Oval, glossy, edged with pale yellow
height	15cm (6in)
planting	In early autumn to early spring
position	Grows almost anywhere but flowers more freely in sun
soil	Ordinary, well-drained garden soil
care	Plants can be cut back hard when necessary
propagation	By division in autumn or spring or by semi-ripe cuttings in midsummer
varieties for flower arranging	*V. m.* has double forms in white and purple; *V. major* 'Elegantissma' is slightly less invasive and has pale purple flowers

FOAM OF MAY
Spiraea × *arguta*

A delightful shrub that flowers profusely, with clusters of tiny flower heads packed tightly together on arching stems. The slender, graceful branches bearing pale green leaves are useful until the autumn when they turn deep yellow.

type	Hardy, deciduous, flowering shrub
flowers	Small, white flowers with yellow centres, tightly clustered on arching stems throughout late spring
foliage	Narrow, oblong, lanceolate, bright green. Useful in arrangements
height	2.5m (8ft)
planting	In mid-autumn to early spring
position	Open, sunny
soil	Fertile soil
care	Thin out occasionally after flowering
propagation	By semi-ripe cuttings in midsummer
varieties for flower arranging	*S. thunbergii* has slightly larger flowers; *S. japonica* 'Gold Flame' has delightful spring foliage – its orange/red/yellow young leaves are its most useful feature to flower arrangers

ORIENTAL POPPY
Papaver orientale 'Salmon Glow'

Poppies are not an obvious choice for flower arranging, but some of the large oriental poppies are spectacular in their markings.

type	Hardy perennial
flowers	Double, salmon-pink flowers
foliage	Fern-like, rough mid-green, not useful for flower arrangements
height	90cm (3ft)
planting	In autumn or spring
position	Sheltered, sunny
soil	Ordinary, well-drained soil
care	Deadhead after flowering. Singe the stem ends of cut flowers to make them last in water (see page 137)
propagation	By seed or by root cuttings (see page 86)
varieties for flower arranging	*P. o.* 'Mrs Perry' has single, salmon flowers; *P. o.* 'Perry's White' has white flowers with purple centres

height	75cm (30in)
planting	Autumn to spring
site	Semi-shade
soil	Fertile, moist, but well-drained
care	Shelter from strong winds, once established do not disturb
propagation	By division in autumn or spring, or by root cuttings in spring
varieties for flower arranging	*Dicentra spectabilis* 'Alba' has delicate white flowers

BLEEDING HEART
Dicentra spectabilis

A very graceful and distinctive plant with delicate flowers which adds an air of elegance to a flower display.

type	Hardy perennial
flowers	Arching sprays of pendent, heart-shaped flowers, which are bi-lobed, red with the inner lobe, white in early to mid summer
foliage	Deeply dissected grey-green foliage, useful for flower arranging, but dies down early in autumn

PLANTAIN LILY
Hosta sieboldiana

Hostas are indispensable for flower arranging, and they are also rewarding plants to grow with their bold sculptural leaves. They disappear altogether for the winter months but compensate for this with their reappearance each spring, vibrant and freshly coloured, as a total surprise.

type	Hardy, clump-forming perennial
flowers	Trumpet-shaped, pale lilac. Not of much use for flower arrangements
foliage	Large, heart-shaped, ribbed leaves of bluish-grey
height	75cm (30in)
planting	In mid-autumn to early spring
position	Light shade, to keep best colour
soil	Moisture-retentive, fertile soil
care	Slug control is usually advisable in early spring
propagation	By division
varieties for flower arranging	*H. fortunei* 'Albopicta' appears early in spring; *H. undulata* has wavy leaves marked with white or silver

practical project *1*

A GARDEN ARRANGEMENT

Arranging flowers out-of-doors seems a bit of a contradiction. In fact, there is often a gap in the garden this month – the main show of bulbs is over and the annuals and bush roses are not yet flowering. The sheltered place for the garden chairs or the tea table may look bare.

Since one of the joys of late spring are the lilac and early climbing roses, transport a few branches and arrange them where they can be appreciated. Cut the top branches of the climbing rose that cannot be seen much any-way, and sprays of lilac from behind the back of the bush. Poppies are included in this arrangement because they flower prolifically. They are not usually brought indoors because of their unpleasant smell. The incredible markings on the inside of the petals can be seen far better in this display than when grow-ing in the border. This is a quick and spontan-eous type of arrangement. It does not need to last much longer than the gathering you are making it for – the special tea or lunch.

MATERIALS

The container

No container is necessary. The soaked oasis can be placed directly on the top of a retaining wall, garden ornament or patio pot. In this instance, the foundation was simply three blocks of soaked oasis, placed directly onto a wall behind a stone seat in an attractive alcove.

Foliage

Foam of May *(Spiraea × arguta)*
Hosta sieboldiana

Flowers

Climbing rose 'Mme. Caroline Testout'
Lilac *(Syringa)*
Poppies 'Perry's White' and 'Salmon Glow'

▪ Cut three long, curving branches of spiraea. Place the tallest to determine the height of the display in proportion to the width and the other two to give a loosely triangular shape. Insert shorter branches to the sides and curving towards the front, keeping within this outline.
▪ Insert three or four very large hostas to the corner and centre of the display (fig 1a).

▪ Remove all the foliage from the lilac (this makes it last longer, see page 137). Add branches of lilac flowers to fill in the outline.
▪ Fill in with long stems of poppies and shorter branches of climbing roses, allowing some of the flowers to droop over the hard edge of the stonework (fig 1b).

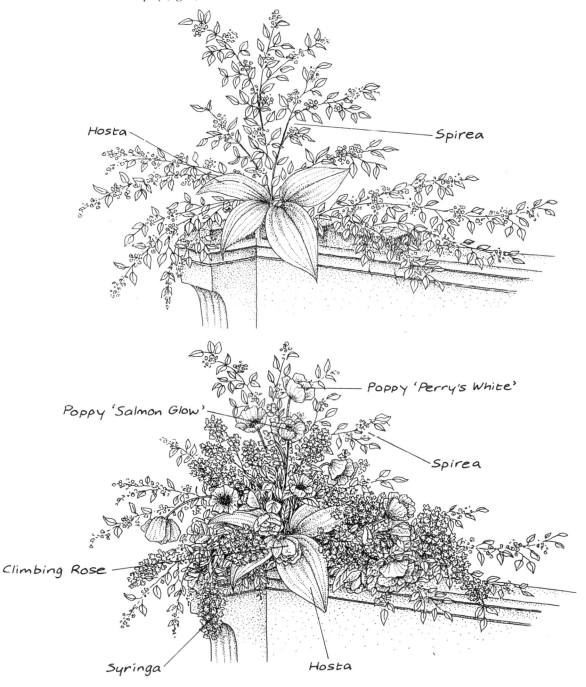

practical project *2*

TUBS AND POTS FOR THE FLOWER ARRANGER

REMEMBER

■ *During the winter, the roots of plants permanently planted in tubs and containers are more susceptible to frost than when they are planted in the open ground. If there is a very severe frost and you cannot move the containers to a frost-free greenhouse, wrap them in insulating material, such as bubble polythene* ■

One tub, brimming with flowers in the corner of a patio, can transform the whole area. A group of tubs, of assorted sizes, some full of flowers and some planted with just a single shrub with a strong outline, can make a complete garden. Arranging patio tubs and pots of different sizes and shapes to form a group and filling them with plants of varying textures, colours and forms is another aspect of flower arranging. The same basic rules apply.

Materials

The containers for the flower arranger are *not* any old stone trough, oil drum, chipped sink or paint can – although, in Mediterranean countries even these can look very pleasing planted with a riot of geraniums. The relationship of the container with the plants is the first thing to catch the flower arranger's eye. Most will opt for wood, terracotta, reconstructed stone, bronze or dull green plastic pots and tubs that will not detract from the flowers. Plastic tubs can get too warm in a sunny corner, and plastic is not such a sympathetic material to look at. Wooden tubs, like driftwood in a flower arrangement, add a rustic dimension and enhance the plants. Terracotta is a reasonably priced, good compromise.

Shapes

The shape of the tub determines how they will best be grouped. Square tubs on short legs are perfect for 'dot' plants – a specimen plant shown in isolation. Large, important-looking, pedestal-type urns are also good for this. Neither of these shapes seems to fit happily into a group. The more usual and very attractive terracotta pots that are frequently sold in garage forecourts as well as plant nurseries, come in all sizes and shapes and are ideal for arranging in groups and combining with other materials. They also blend in happily which stone paths, gravel drives, modern paving slabs, stone setts, or even tarmac.

Grouping

The group should be an odd number – three, five and so on, and placed, if possible, at different heights. The height of the actual containers can be varied by placing some on a step or terrace, or by placing one on a plinth, a wrought iron base or upturned terracotta saucer. It also makes a far more pleasing group to combine at least three different container shapes. An interesting arrangement could incorporate a closed shape, such as a water-pot or oil-jar shape, combined with the traditional flower-pot shape. A fairly low, shallow open bowl at the front will draw the eye downwards

to provide a 'full stop' and add interest to the group. The low bowl is ideal for a bright splash of winter-flowering pansies when summer planting is finished and you can look down on their faces in wintertime.

Sizes

Include also a few different sizes. As with an arrangement of flowers, a very large pot placed next to a small one will not make a satisfying combination. It needs a third pot of an intermediate size to make the transition between the two and unify the group.

Compost

What you use to fill the tubs is vital to the health of the plants. Closely planted in a container they will have to compete for nutrients. They will also need to be watered frequently while water-logged soil is death to plants. So a compost that is free-draining and yet holds sufficient water to provide moisture and feeding is essential. If you fill the tubs with garden soil you run the risk of including garden pests. It also tends to become too compact. It is better to buy clean compost. As with seed-sowing you have a choice between peat- or coir-based compost and soil-based compost. Whichever type you choose, buy compost specifically made for containers. The label will specify the most appropriate use – 'seed and cutting compost' and 'potting compost'.

This grouping of patio tubs is in a sheltered area of my own garden. They are all permanently planted in potting compost.

THE FIRST TUB

Eucalyptus gunnii provides a constant supply of blue-grey foliage. In the autumn much of it is preserved with glycerine. It is cut down completely in early spring and the new growth of perfoliate leaves begins to appear almost at once. **Lilies 'Casa Blanca'** are permanently planted in the same tub. *Euonymus* **'Cannadale Gold'** trails over the side of the tub. This has large leaves with gold and white splashes.

THE SECOND TUB

Phormium tenax **'Yellow Wave'** is the only occupant of the oil-jar-shaped tub and it is a satisfying shape to look at. Unlike the upright common phormium, which also grows well at the seaside, it has a curved, weeping leaf, yellow when young, developing green-striped variation as it matures. Well worth searching for.

**MINIATURE ROSES
FOR CONTAINERS**
(see also pages 59, 71)

'Darling Flame' – bright orange
with gold shading
'Dresden Doll' – shell-pink, gold
stamens
'Little Flirt' – double orange-red
with yellow reverse
'Masquerade' – yellow buds,
changing to pink and red
New Penny – coppery salmon
pink

**PATIO ROSES FOR
CONTAINERS**
(see also pages 59, 71)

'Avon' – glossy foliaged, pale pink
buds, opening to white double
blooms, spreads more widely
than most, 60–90cm
(2–3ft)
'Boy's Brigade' – crimson, prolific
flowerer
'Clair Scotland' – apricot, bushy,
compact
'Dainty Dinah' – coral-pink,
compact
'Gingernut' – bronze-orange with
red reverse, double
'Peek-a-Boo' apricot or pink sprays
of small flowers, compact
'Ray of Sunshine' – bushy, small
leaves, semi-double, yellow
blooms
'The Fairy' – dainty sprays of pink
flowers, small glossy leaves
'Wee Jock' – scarlet crimson,
compact, prolific flowerer

THE THIRD TUB

These trailing geraniums are lifted from the
shallow bowl each year and brought inside for
cuttings for next year. The annuals included
vary from year to year, but the trailing variegated catmint *(Nepeta hederacea* 'Variegata') is a
permanent fixture.

THE FOURTH TUB

Curry plant (*Helichrysum serotinum*) is a
satisfying, tufty, silver-grey plant that blends
comfortably with the **Euonymus 'Emerald**

Gaiety' in the tub below. This isn't emerald at
all, but a small grey-green leaf, edged with
white. The white alyssum is self-seeded and
not a flower arranger's plant at all, but it
provides a colour link between the greys and
the white-edged euonymus. **Creeping Jenny
(*Lysimachia nummularia* 'Aurea')** dies down
completely over the winter.

THE FIFTH TUB

The patio rose 'Sweet Magic' gains some
shelter over the winter from the nearby wall
and from the proximity of the other tubs. A
trailing, annual edging plant is often added
into this pot as well, in this case trailing lobelia.

plants
OF THE
month

PROPAGATING LILAC

Lilac can be propagated from the suckers that it produces in abundance. However, since the best of the lilacs are grafted plants, any new shrub grown this way won't have the attractive typical characteristics of the grafted bush. It will have the properties of the rootstock. Lilac propagated from cuttings taken now from a grafted bush will have the same properties. Find the place where new growth has started from the old wood. Cut off a new shoot cleanly with a sharp knife, about 8cm (3in) long.

Remove the lower leaves and dip the end into hormone rooting powder.

Insert into a pot of cuttings compost. Water lightly. Provide humidity and shade as for softwood cuttings (see page 86).

COMMON LILAC
Syringa vulgaris

Evocative of cottage gardens and heady summer days, a mass of lilac flowers need very little in the way of arranging. All the foliage should be removed so that the flowers last longer.

type	Hardy deciduous shrub or small tree
flowers	Fragrant panicles of small tubular flowers in spring
foliage	Mid-green, dull, ovate leaves of little use in flower arranging
height	Up to 4m (12ft)
planting	Autumn
site	Sun or part shade
soil	Fertile well-drained, preferably alkaline
care	Remove flowerheads from newly planted lilacs, dead head for the first few years
propagation	Semi-hardwood cuttings in summer
varieties for flower arranging	*S. v.* 'Firmament' is the one we all think of as 'lilac'. Pinkish-tinged in bud, it opens to pure lavender/lilac. *S. v.* 'Blue Hyacinth' is a spreading shrub with graceful arching branches of pale lilac blue flowers; *S.* 'Primrose' has creamy-yellow flowers on a bushy shrub and is only slightly scented

CORN LILIES
Ixia hybrids

Although quite delightful flowers for arranging, unfortunately *Ixia* are not reliably hardy, but they are inexpensive and can be replaced annually.

type	Corms
flowers	Six-petalled, star-shaped flowers in a variety of attractive colours with contrasting centres in spring or summer

foliage	Mid-green, spear-shaped leaves
height	40cm (16in)
planting	In mild areas plant the corms 5cm (2in) deep in autumn for spring flower, or in spring for later summer flowers
site	Sunny, sheltered
soil	Ordinary, well-drained
care	Protect from frost
propagation	By offsets

CLIMBING ROSE

Rosa 'Mme. Caroline Testout'

A climbing sport of *R.* 'Mme Caroline Testout', which was introduced in 1901. Grow it against a wall to enjoy the heady experience of looking up into the large, soft pink cabbage-type blooms, nodding from sturdy branches. These roses make a voluptuous focal point in any display.

type	Climbing large-flowered (hybrid tea) rose
flowers	Rose-pink, full-double, slight scent in summer
foliage	Dull mid-green
height	Up to 6m (20ft)
planting	Autumn or spring
site	Full sun
soil	Fertile, rich, free-draining
care	If grown against a wall, water during dry periods
propagation	By semi-hardwood cuttings
varieties for flower arranging	*R.* 'New Dawn' has small, double heads of delicate blush-pink with a long flowering period; *R.* 'Compassion' has large double apricot-pink blooms with excellent dark green glossy foliage; *R.* 'Aloha' has large, well-shaped, rose-pink blooms. Climbs only 2m (6ft) approx; *R.* 'Breath of Life' bears abundant, large, apricot blooms. Long lasting indoors and one of the best climbers for flower arranging. Delicate scent; *R.* 'Golden Showers' with bright yellow, semi-double blooms is good displayed on its own in a copper-coloured bowl; *R.* 'High Hopes' bears abundant clusters of medium-sized blooms of clear, light pink. Excellent foliage for cutting and preserving in glycerine. Sweetly scented. *(See page 71 for more roses)*

J U N E

*This is the month of roses – and for me roses are the supreme
flowers for arranging. If it were not for the garden roses, flower
arranging would lose much of its appeal. The full-blown hybrid
garden rose and the sprawling clusters of the old-fashioned rose
are enchanting and bear very little resemblance to the tight, thin-
stemmed florist's rosebuds.*

*It is probably the month that gives gardeners the most gratification
and flower arrangers the most scope. The long hours of daylight
and increasing sunshine give the plants the necessary energy for
rapid growth and flower production, and it is a joy to watch the
daily changes in the garden as the plants open and the flowers
unfold. The long evenings are a real delight, not only to work in
the garden, but for an evening stroll among the shrubs and flower
beds checking on new varieties we may have tried out and colour
schemes which are new this year. If only gardening were always
like this! Tender plants we have been coddling can now go
outdoors – we would have to be very unfortunate to get frost this
month. Dahlias, nerines, geraniums, bedding plants and the
hardier indoor plants – all can be planted outside in lavish excess.
This is also the month with the longest days, when the sun should
be at its strongest. The soil often dries out quickly now, and this is
why we need to be even more regular in giving nature a bit of a
hand by feeding and watering. Sweet peas, in particular, should
not be allowed to dry out, and roses also perform better if they are
kept well watered. Climbers and ramblers on house walls are
particularly prone to dry out this month as the walls warm up in
the sunshine. After watering the plants in the evening, it is
immensely satisfying to take time off and sit near the roses to
appreciate them and the other scents of evening.*

tasks

FOR THE

month

PLANT FOODS

MAJOR NUTRIENTS
Nitrogen • Phosphorus •
Potassium • Calcium •
Magnesium • Sulphur •
Carbon • Oxygen • Hydrogen

**MINOR NUTRIENTS OR
TRACE ELEMENTS**
Iron • Manganese • Boron
Copper • Zinc • Molybdenum

ORGANIC FERTILISERS
Dried blood • Blood, fish and bone
Garden lime – a natural mineral
Bonemeal • Hoof and horn

CHECKLIST

- ☑ Feed plants by adding organic or inorganic fertilisers to the soil
- ☑ Mulch ground thoroughly around flowers
- ☑ Water all plants regularly and thoroughly
- ☑ Deadhead annuals, bedding plants and shrubs unless grown for their seed heads
- ☑ Stake tall plants

MAINTENANCE

FEEDING PLANTS

This month plants make a great deal of growth, and most will benefit from additional feeding. The nutrients they draw from the soil need to be replaced to get the best blooms and to encourage a longer succession of flowers.

Plant foods are divided into two main groups: major and minor nutrients. Minor nutrients are not so called because they are less *important* than the others. They are grouped according to the *amount* of each that the plant needs. The most important elements, which plants require in large amounts, are nitrogen, phosphorus and potassium. It is vital to the successful cultivation of plants to have all these elements present in the correct amounts and available throughout the life-cycle of the plant.

Nitrogen (N)

Nitrogen encourages healthy leaf growth, strongly growing stems and new shoots. It gives the leaves a good green colour by providing chlorophyll which it needs to convert the energy from the sun. *Too much* nitrogen, in relation to the other elements, produces an abundance of soft, weak foliage at the expense of flowers. It also makes the plant more prone to disease.

Too little nitrogen results in yellowing of the leaves and premature leaf fall in some cases. Growth is stunted.

Phosphorus (P) (phosphate)

This nutrient encourages root growth, early maturity and helps the plant's resistance to disease. It needs to be incorporated in the soil before planting. *Too little* phosphorus results in red or purple leaves. The growth of the plant is retarded, and it is susceptible to disease and cold weather.

Potassium (K) (potash)

Potassium creates sturdy growth, good flowers and healthy fruit. *Too little* produces stunted growth and pale yellow or brown mottling of the leaves.

MULCHING

A mulch is a top dressing of organic material that is spread over the surface of the soil to retain moisture and to inhibit the growth of weeds. Some mulching materials also supply nutrients. They decompose and can be dug in during autumn and so will improve the structure of the soil.

Mulching should be done early in the month, when the soil is damp, after any feeding has been applied to the soil and before the hot dry days to come.

Well-rotted manure, mushroom compost, straw, peat and soil-conditioning peat substitutes, chipped bark, coconut fibre, leaf-mould and compost are all good for mulching.

Which to use

If you are mulching a flower bed or rose bed on view from the house, you obviously won't want rotted manure on top of the bed – although very early in the year this would be a splendid item to

---

CHOICE OF FERTILISER

Necessary nutrients can be added to the soil by organic matter, such as well-rotted manure, or by fertilisers, which themselves can be of chemical or organic origin.

Organic fertilisers

These are derived from animal and plant sources, are slow acting and, apart from dried blood, remain in the soil, so are available to the plant over a long period. It is a good idea to add bone meal to the planting medium for every newly planted shrub. Slow-release organic fertilisers are not sufficient in the long term or for vigorously growing plants, so a top dressing of a fertiliser is necessary, usually once a year, in spring.

Inorganic fertilisers

These are fast acting and good for regular applications over the growing period. There are dozens of brands on the market. Read the labels on the packets to decide which one you need. The ratio of nitrogen to phosphorus to potassium contained in them is given. For example, a general fertiliser for flowers and shrubs, vegetables and fruit is labelled N P K 7 7 7; a proprietary flower fertiliser is labelled N P K 5.3 7.5 10. Here the comparatively low nitrogen content and the very high potassium content means that the plant will not produce leaves at the expense of flowers, which it would if treated with a general fertiliser. There is a balanced fertiliser for every plant type.

use. For 'cosmetic' reasons a mulch of chipped bark is a good choice for a rose bed at this later time of year. It looks good and does a good job of suppressing weeds and conserving moisture.

How to apply

First remove all visible weeds by hand. Choose a day when the soil is thoroughly damp or water it well, then spread the bark to a thickness of 5-8cm (2-3in) over the surface of the soil. The mulch should not be disturbed throughout the summer. It can be dug in during autumn and will add bulk to the soil.

WATERING

It has been estimated that on a hot summer's day every square metre of leaf cover in the garden can lose 5 litres of water through evaporation. If there is no rain, plants in tubs will die and those in the flower beds will not give of their best. Only plants like alpines and rockery plants will thrive. Strong flower stems and lush foliage for flower arranging will be scarce.

To reduce the need for watering add plenty of organic material to the soil on a regular basis, to newly prepared borders in particular and to any beds left empty over the winter. Use a mulch on all borders at the right time (see mulching). Select those plants which have the most chance of surviving in the drier areas in your garden.

Plants must be watered *thoroughly* – a light sprinkling of the surface soil does more harm than good. It encourages the plant to send roots upwards towards the soil surface, searching for more water. A thorough watering once a week is better than a skimpy one every few days. See margin for watering tips.

PLANT CARE

Deadheading

This is the term used for the removal of dying flowers from the plant. It must be done on a regular basis, not only to improve the look of the garden, but to prevent a plant setting seed. The idea behind deadheading is to convince the plant it has many more flowering days ahead and to conserve its energy for future growth and the production of flowers. Deadhead all annuals, bedding plants and shrubs regularly, unless they are grown especially for their seed heads.

Staking

Many herbaceous plants and annuals have put on considerable growth by the middle of this month and need to be staked or tied to a support. The best way is to provide for this *before* they reach that stage.

• For bushy annuals such as argyranthemums (*Chrysanthemum frutescens*) or cosmos, push twiggy sticks of brushwood (hazel) or birch into the ground

around the plants when you transplant them into their permanent positions. Snap the tops of any tall twigs and bend them over so that the plant will grow through them.

• For bushy herbaceous perennials with delicate stems that tend to be felled by the wind, such as oriental poppies, push in a group of

tall canes and tie with green garden twine around and criss-crossing the canes so that the plants will grow up through the twine.

• For tall spikes of plants such as delphiniums or border chrysanthemums insert a single tall bamboo cane at the back of the individual plant. Tie the stem to the cane with soft green twine in a figure of eight to keep stake and stem apart.

• Use 'Canemates', which consist of three flexible sleeves joined together, for making tripods from canes for sweet peas, or a frame to support any other tall-growing plants.

BASIC WATERING EQUIPMENT

Choose a tough hose and attach it to the outdoor tap with a leak-proof tap connector.

Various tools can be fitted to the end of the hose with a hose connector. The best type will allow you to shut off the water at the hose end. You can get a tool with various kinds of spray for different tasks or use a sprinkler, which, when fitted with an Aquameter water controller, will switch it off when it has finished watering. A hose end feeder combines both watering and feeding.

NOTE

Shrubs should not be fed after midsummer or they will produce new soft growth which will be damaged in winter.

PLANTS TO DEADHEAD

Camellias • Delphiniums • Lilac • Rhododendrons • Roses • Sweet peas

PLANTS NOT TO DEADHEAD

**Alliums
Chinese lanterns (*Physalis*)
Clematis
Giant cornflower (*Centaurea macrocephela*)
Honesty (*Lunaria*)
Love-in-a-mist (*Nigella*)
Pampas grass (*Cortaderia*)
Poppy
Teasel (*Dipsacus fullonum*)**

plants
OF THE
month

SNAPDRAGON

Antirrhinum majus 'White Spire'

This is one of the oldest garden flowers, and it is now available in a range of wonderful colours. One of the most useful varieties for flower arranging is this creamy white one. Cultivars also vary greatly in height – good news for the flower arranger, as the longer-stemmed snapdragons are invaluable.

type	Annual
flowers	Spikes of creamy-white, trumpet-shaped single flowers
foliage	Pointed, slender, oval leaves of little interest for flower arranging
height	20–75cm (8–30in)
planting	Under glass in early spring. Plant out when all danger of frost has passed
position	Full sun to light shade
soil	Well-drained, fertile soil
care	Pinch out growing point to encourage branching. Feed during season
propagation	From seed
varieties for flower arranging	'Coronet Mixed'

MEADOW RUE

Thalictrum flavum 'Glauca'

This golden meadow rue is as useful to the flower arranger as *Alchemilla mollis* for both its flowers and its foliage. Although its height restricts where it can be grown, it is invaluable for adding a touch of old fashioned delicacy to a posy of flowers or formal display.

type	Clump-forming perennial
flowers	Small, fluffy clusters of stamens with four to five sepals in mid-summer
foliage	Bipinnate, glaucous, blue-green leaves
height	1.2-1.5m (4-5ft)
planting	Autumn to spring
site	Best colour in sun but will tolerate light shade
soil	Thrives best in rich moist soil
care	Stake before the plant grows too tall. Cut down when foliage can no longer be used. Feed with general fertiliser in spring
propagation	Seed or by division in spring, slow to establish
varieties for flower arranging	T. f. 'Illuminator', pale yellow fluffy heads, bright green foliage

GOLDEN PRIVET

Ligustrum ovalifolium 'Aureo-marginatum'

Neglected varieties covered in city grime can prejudice us to the real beauty of this plant. If it is well grown, however, it is a spectacular shrub – the new growth is limey-green, edged with pale yellow and invaluable for flower arrangers. It can be grown easily in a patio tub.

type	Hardy evergreen
flowers	Insignificant
foliage	Ovate, glossy, bright green edged with yellow. Invaluable for flower arranging
height	4m (12ft)
planting	Mid-autumn to mid-spring
position	Sun or shade
soil	Ordinary garden soil
care	Cut back in late winter to get best leaf colour for flower arranging
propagation	By hardwood cuttings in mid-autumn
varieties for flower arranging	The leaves of 'Aureo-marginatum' Variegatum' are edged with a pale creamy yellow

JAMAICA PRIMROSE

Argyranthemum frutescens
(often known as *Chrysanthemum frutescens*)

Reminiscent of childhood and daisy chains, this is a delightful flower. Both the white (Paris daisy) and yellow varieties of Jamaica primrose are showy and eye-catching in patio tubs or in the border.

type	Tender, evergreen, bushy perennial
flowers	Daisy-type, bright yellow flowers that fade slightly as they age. Long-flowering, from early summer till the first frost
foliage	Deeply dissected, fresh, green
height	45-75cm (18-30in)
planting	Early summer, after danger of frost has passed
position	Full sun
soil	Ordinary, light garden soil
care	Feed lightly during the flowering season, deadhead during the summer. May survive the winter if very sheltered. Cut down in spring
propagation	By semi-ripe cuttings in midsummer. Over-winter under glass
varieties for flower arranging	*A. f.* 'Vancouver' has pink flowers; *A. f.* 'Paris White' has bright, daisy-type flowers

STEPHANANDRA

Stephanandra incisa 'Crispa'

A delightful shrub for the flower arranger with arching branches of very attractive foliage throughout the summer and beautiful autumn tints; it is also very easy to grow.

type	Deciduous, summer-flowering shrub
flowers	Tiny, star-shaped, greenish white flowers in early summer
foliage	Ovate, deeply incised, crinkly, turning yellow in autumn
height	1.5cm (5ft)
planting	Mid-autumn to early spring
position	Sun or part shade
soil	Ordinary, well-drained soil
care	Cut back older wood after flowering
propagation	By rooted suckers or division in autumn, or by semi-ripe cuttings in summer
varieties for flower arranging	*S. tanakae* is taller, growing to over 3m (10ft), and has larger leaves; *S. i. prostrata* is a low, arching form that can be used as groundcover, on a rockery. Trim back when it gets too rampant. Spread to about 1.2m (4ft)

practical project *1*

'SUMMER BUFFET'

YOU WILL NEED
two rounds of oasis foam
florist's thin, green tape

This flower arrangement is the essence of summer. Meadow-type flowers and airy green foliage with ribbons of organza surround a basket of summer produce. It is an easy arrangement to make for a summer party. By making two almost identical arrangements you can create a sense of occasion without losing the charm and informality of the flowers.

MATERIALS

The containers
Two Venetian glass stemmed vases. Any footed containers will achieve the same effect of lightness – empty, clear or green glass bottles can be converted into flower holders by using a candle cup (see page 32).

Foliage
Stephanandra incisa
Golden privet (*Ligustrum ovalifolium* 'Aureo-marginatum')
Hosta fortunei 'Albopicta'

Flowers
Snapdragon (*Antirrhinum* 'White Spire')
Jamaica Primrose (*Chrysanthemum frutescens* also known as *Argyranthemum frutescens*)
Meadow rue (*Thalictrum flavum* 'Glauca')

■ Work with both flower arrangements at the same time to achieve a similarity between the two.

■ For each one, wedge the soaked oasis in the cup of the container so that it projects at least 5cm (2in) above the rim. Wrap the thin tape around the cup to hold it securely.

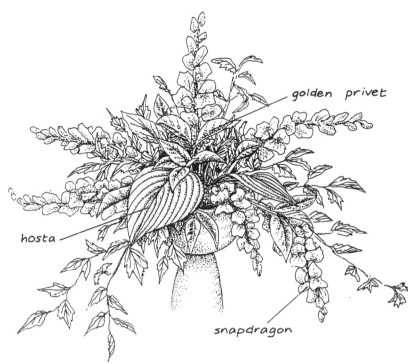

- Insert a central branch of the small-leaved stephanandra in the centre of the oasis. This will be the finished height of the arrangement. Insert trailing branches to each side, then longer ones flowing downwards to outline a loose triangular shape (fig 1a).
- Keep within this outline and add short sprigs of privet, and a few large hosta leaves to the centre. Insert foliage from all sides to achieve an all-round display.
- Add stems of white snapdragon, following the outline, allowing some to trail downwards and others to reach out to the sides and top of the foliage outline. Shorten a few stems to add towards the centre (fig 1b).
- Add the yellow argyranthemums, making their stems a little shorter than the snapdragons.
- Finally add sprigs of meadow rue throughout the design to soften it (fig 1c).

practical project *2*

A WEDDING BOUQUET

YOU WILL NEED

florist's reel wire (56mm gauge)
two 'Wedding Belle' holders
florist's wire
florist's stem tape (gutta percha)

WET FOAM OASIS HOLDERS
The disadvantage of these holders is that whereas they hold the flower stem very firmly once it is put in, they do not allow two or three goes at it, without making holes in the foam and loosening its grip so you cannot experiment. The way round this is to buy two holders and make one bouquet the day before, to make sure you know what you are doing then make a duplicate early in the morning of the day it is needed.

HANDLE
The handle of the 'Wedding Belle' can be wound with ribbon.

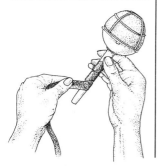

These days, wedding bouquets are not the heavily wired contraptions they used to be and not all weddings are formal occasions. For a simple wedding or an anniversary party it is quite possible to make an attractive presentation bouquet of garden flowers.

Recently, a new oasis foam holder has been introduced – a 'Wedding Belle'. Using this, making a simple bouquet is possible for the experienced flower arranger. Previously, a bouquet was made up of individually wired flowers; these were then wired and taped into groups and then the groups were wired together, making rather a heavy bouquet. Dry foam was introduced next to save time on wiring. Well-conditioned flowers last reasonably well in a dry foam holder, but it is still a task for a florist. Now a wet foam holder is available, and for the flower arranger wanting to have a go at floristry it is ideal.

MATERIALS

Foliage
Small-leaved ivy

Flowers
Astilbe × arendsii
Lady's mantle *(Alchemilla mollis)*
Sweet peas
Rosa 'New Dawn'
Pinks *(Dianthus)*
Bleeding heart *(Dicentra spectabile* 'Alba')

- First condition the flowers and foliage well (see page 137). Use an empty bottle to hold the oasis holder, to leave both hands for working.
- Immerse the oasis on the holder for about 15 seconds in water. Soaking too long means the foam will drip water.
- Establish the approximate length and shape of the bouquet. The easiest for the beginner is the egg shape – the traditional shower bouquet, with two thirds of the flowers below the holder and one third above (fig 2a).

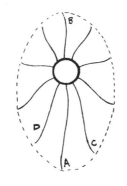

- Cut a long trail of ivy to the main length A. This stem is the most vulnerable part of the bouquet and, although it is not essential, it is a good idea to secure it with wire. Cut a wire to the length of the spray of ivy plus 12cm (5in). Wind the wire between the ivy leaves, close to the stem (fig 2b).

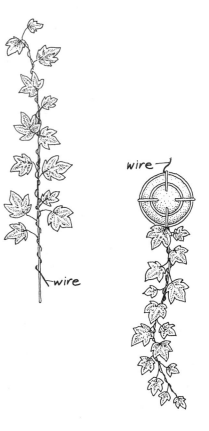

- Push wire and stem through the oasis at the base and against the frame. Bring the surplus wire out at the other side and hook the end around the frame to secure it (fig 2c).
- Support the holder in the neck of an empty bottle, to leave both hands free. Make the outline with lengths of ivy B, C and D in the same way. No further wiring is needed. Complete the outline with the foliage as in the diagram 2a (fig 2d).
- Cut the astilbe to very short lengths and push these into the oasis at the base of the frame. Add slightly longer lengths following the outline (fig 2e). The stems are pushed deep into the foam, deeper than is usually necessary.
- Add short sprigs of lady's mantle to give a rounded outline to the bouquet. Look at the shape from the sides to establish good outline. (fig 2f).

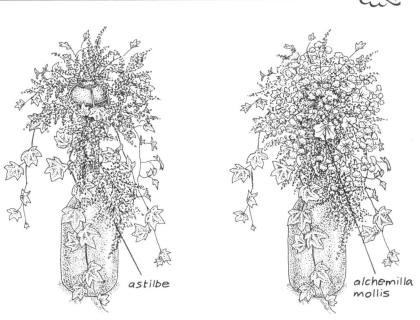

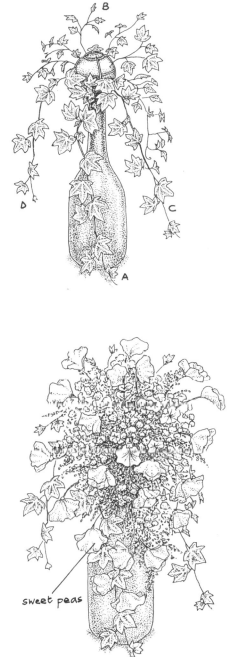

- Add sweet peas cutting the stem lengths to follow this 'egg' shape. Insert each stem pointing to the imaginary centre of the bouquet (fig 2g).
- Add the roses, varying the stem lengths. Include a few pinks to strengthen the silhouette and a few stems of bleeding heart to produce graceful curves.

practical project *2*

A WEDDING BUTTONHOLE

YOU WILL NEED

florist's green stem wire
gutta percha tape

This is simple to make once you have the stem wire, using a garden rose.

MATERIALS

Foliage
Rose foliage in perfect condition
Asparagus fern from a houseplant
(Asparagus plumosus)

Flowers
A single well-formed small rose and rose bud

- Wire the rose head and bud separately by inserting the wire through the calyx and twisting the ends together and around the stem (fig 3a).

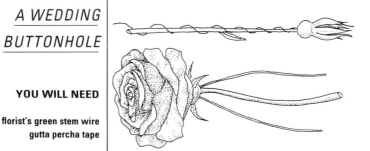

- Wire the rose leaf by taking a 'stitch' through the back of the leaf and twisting the ends around the stem (fig 3b).
- Wire the rose and bud. Arrange them with the foliage as a backing and wire together (fig 3c).
- Wrap the stems with gutta percha and trim to the desired length.

plants
OF THE
month

Rose classification
Roses are officially classified into three groups: species, old garden and modern. Within the old garden group and the modern group there are many other sub-divisions.

Wild roses – Species roses, or any that resemble species roses
Old garden roses – All those roses that belong to a class of rose in common use before the introduction of the hybrid tea rose
Modern garden roses – All the new varieties
   These three divisions are subdivided into climbing and non-climbing. The modern garden roses are subdivided again into recurrent flowering and non-recurrent flowering, and again into large-flowered bush roses (hybrid tea) or cluster-flowered bush roses (floribunda).

The choice in rose catalogues
Species roses are the roses that grow in their original wild form and have a lax, shrubby habit of growth. Their flowers are single (dog roses) and they flower only once a year.

Shrub roses are sometimes subdivided into old shrub roses and modern shrub roses, largely for reasons of pruning. **Old shrub roses** are descendants of *Rosa × alba* (the white rose of York), the cabbage rose, and the Damask rose.

'Madame Hardy' is one of the best, a wonderfully evocative rose to be near on a warm evening. It has sumptuous, large flowers like camellias in midsummer and good glossy foliage for flower arranging.

Modern shrub roses are mainly hybrids between wild species roses and hybrid teas and floribundas. They are many and varied, flowering intermittently throughout the summer.

Hybrid tea roses (large-flowered bush) are, in their most perfect form, centuries removed from the wild dog rose. In the process of refining, they have lost some of its scent, its fragility and daintiness and acquired a much tidier almost sculptured look.

Floribunda roses (cluster-flowered bush) are less popular for flower arranging as the flowers are in terminal clusters and the stems not as long as the hybrid tea. In the garden, these roses fit in well in a mixed or herbaceous border. The modern floribunda rose has large flowers and does not need to be disbudded.

Low-growing and patio roses (dwarf cluster-flowered bush roses) are now offered by most nurseries and are ideal for the rose lover without much space. Roses do well in tubs as long as they are not allowed to dry out and are fed regularly. Miniature roses can be planted as the main feature, singly or in a group of three, in a large tub with low-growing trailing plants around the edges, or are excellent for mixing with evergreen or other less colourful permanent planting in patio pots. There are many varieties, all of them growing to around 30cm (12in). (See p57.) Although not much use for cutting they are perfect for wedding buttonholes.

Patio roses are low-growing, free-flowering floribunda types, recommended for tubs by growers. They grow larger than miniature roses, 30–45cm (12–18in), and can hold their own in a planting scheme – giving a wider choice of companion plants.

Groundcover roses are low growing, widely spreading shrubs that hug the ground. They have healthy, attractive foliage and are not only excellent for groundcover and keeping down weeds, but the long branches are useful as foliage in an arrangement as it is produced in abundance.

Climbers and ramblers have always seemed to me the perfect flower arrangement, loose, tumbling, delicate with an airy charm that is lost as soon as they are anchored in a vase. But although they never look as charming indoors as they do on the bush, they still transform a room when their arching stems are shown against a plain wall.

ROSES FOR FLOWER ARRANGING

SPECIES ROSES

Rosa glauca (which used to be known as *Rosa rubrifolia*) – grown for its grey-green foliage and scarlet hips in autumn. The flowers are unremarkable

Rosa × 'Canary Bird' – an early flowerer with clear yellow dog roses and attractive ferny foliage all year, black hips in autumn

Rosa moyesii 'Geranium' – a glowing red dog rose flowering sport of *Rosa moyesii*. Very large, bottle-shaped hips in autumn, not as prolific as *R. moyesii*, for the smaller garden

SHRUB ROSES

'Nevada' – grows strongly, is smothered in cascades of creamy-white single blooms with yellow stamens, almost thornless foliage

'Constance Spry' – grows strongly as a wall shrub or a bush, with spectacular, large, very fragrant double flowers of a clear pink, flowers only once

HYBRID TEAS

'Alexander' – brilliant vermilion red, tall, strong grower, good foliage which glycerines well

'Corso' – pure orange flame, very long lasting as a cut flower

'Fyvie Castle' – perfect form and wonderful light apricot, shaded amber and pink, glossy foliage

'Peace' – tall grower, large blooms of golden yellow edged with vivid pink, opening to shades of ivory and cream

'Silver Jubilee' – remarkably disease-resistant and free-flowering, blooms of perfect form in shades of pink, apricot and cream

'Grandpa Dickson' – straight, and vigorous in growth, free-flowering with clear yellow blooms maturing to creamy-yellow tinged with green and pink

'Summer Fragrance' – deep velvety red blooms, strong grower and glossy dark green foliage

FLORIBUNDA ROSES

'Glenfiddich' – golden-amber, well-shaped, double, fragrant blooms, vigorous upright growth, dark green foliage, repeat-flowering.

'Korresia' – bushy with double yellow, tea-shaped flowers that do not fade, fragrant, good foliage

'Queen Elizabeth' – extremely vigorous, height up to 2m (6ft 6in), long stems without thorns, well-shaped, clear pink blooms with slight fragrance

'Mountbatten' – mimosa-yellow flowers of rounded form, fragrant, good foliage

'Memento' – salmon-vermilion, neat, double flowers, slight fragrance

'Rob Roy' – large hybrid tea-type flowers of deep red, upright and vigorous

'Oranges and Lemons' – copper-coloured foliage in early spring, blooms opening to striped scarlet and lemon, upright, vigorous, slight fragrance

GROUNDCOVER ROSES

'Max Graf' – makes a dense groundcover of long, trailing shoots with bright green leaves, horrific thorns, can only be handled with gloves, long lasting and attractive as background foliage, dog-rose deep pink flowers, not suitable for cutting

'Bonica' – spreading, arching, shrubby growth, with cascades of soft pink double blooms, orange hips in autumn

CLIMBERS AND RAMBLERS

'Albertine' – sprays of coppery pink blooms

'New Dawn' – nearly pink blooms of utter delicacy

'Compassion' – perfectly formed flower heads in clusters of apricot pink

'Leaping Salmon' – well-formed hybrid tea-type blooms, excellent dark green glossy foliage

JULY

Midsummer – the month of sweet peas, pinks *and* roses *and a
wealth of annual flowers and foliage plants to choose from in the
garden. Many of the commoner flowering shrubs have one of their
varieties in flower at this time of year –* honeysuckle, clematis,
broom, viburnum *are just a few. Foliage is at its best, either
shimmering in the sun or shedding raindrops. Green foliage has
outgrown its tender spring leaves and is sturdy and long lasting.
Hostas are plentiful with long stems and mature, tough leaves –
an ideal focal point of large arrangements. The grey foliage of*
senecio, artemesia *and* cineraria *is abundant.*

*For me this is the month that makes all the work in the garden
worthwhile and nor is effort, care, thought. Whichever word you
use for the pleasurable planning and toil that goes into making a
garden, this is the month for my favourite arrangement – a basket
of roses and sweet peas; sometimes garden pinks are included as
well. Pinks and feathery grey artemesia together in a small clear
glass bowl are another breathtaking combination this month. But
it is the basket of roses filling the empty hearth which is the chief
delight. The long evenings mean we can take a more leisurely
attitude to gardening and, given a run of warm days, this is the
time to enjoy harvesting the annuals you grew especially for
drying. Pick them over several weeks, while they are in peak
condition. Dried flowers can sometimes be uninteresting. To
counteract this, dry a succession of blooms at different stages of
development and include as many varieties and different shapes,
colours and foliages as you can. Although with a dried
arrangement you will never achieve that special elusive charm of
living flowers, they are an asset when flowers and foliage are
scarce and a satisfying reminder of your garden in summertime.*

tasks
FOR THE
month

ABUNDANT BLOOMS
Climbing roses growing straight upwards tend to flower only at the top. Tie in the new shoots to grow horizontally, or as near as is practicable, and this will encourage flowering shoots along the entire length. Train roses grown up a pillar so that they spiral around it and this will produce the same result.

PERENNIAL EVERLASTINGS FOR FLOWER ARRANGING

Anaphilis – pearly everlasting, grey foliage, clusters of tiny white flowers
Carlina acaulis – thistle-type silvery-white flower, pull out the seeds from the centre
***(Limonium bonduelli)* Statice** – mixed colours as well as the traditional purple
***(Physalis franchetii)* Chinese orange lanterns**

CHECKLIST

- Check your stock of roses and plan for new ones
- Increase your stock of carnations by layering
- Harvest flowers for drying

PLANNING

ROSES

Roses are at their best this month – they tumble from trellises, climb up stone walls and fences, wave around corners and stand up smartly in public parks. This is the time to look round at all the different types of roses and to choose new varieties to order for autumn planting.

The real rose lover is expected to prefer the old shrub roses, but to most flower arrangers any rose is a sheer delight. The old roses can add a country garden touch and a softness to an arrangement. The modern rose with its more constrained and sculptured appearance can bring a quality of elegance and dignity. (See p.71 for more about roses.)

NOTE

■ *A sucker on a rose is a shoot that comes from below the budding union of the rose. You may first notice its leaf formation, which is different from that of the main bush. Follow it back and you will find that it comes out from the rootstock. Sever it at that point or it will produce many more and the rose will eventually revert to the rootstock ■*

PROPAGATION

LAYERING BORDER CARNATIONS

Carnations and pinks grow straggly in their second and third year. They can be renewed very easily by layering shoots from the parent plant in the border where they grow.

■ Choose a healthy vigorous shoot and remove the leaves from the lower section, leaving about four or five fully developed pairs of leaves.
■ Make a clean oblique cut with a knife, just below the lowest leaves, cutting along the centre of the stem and slitting through the leaf joint below it (fig 1).
■ Open out the slit, leaving a tongue (fig 2) and dust this lightly with hormone rooting powder using a paint brush.
■ Bend the shoot down to the soil, keeping the cut open and just below the soil. Bury its length to a depth of 2.5cm (1in) and secure it with a bent wire (fig 3).
■ After six or seven weeks, when roots have formed, sever it from the parent plant.
■ Dig out the old unwanted plant, leaving the new plants to grow on until a good root system has formed and after this they can then be moved.
■ Once the plant has made several pairs of leaves, pinch out the tops to encourage bushy growth (fig 4a & b).

fig 1

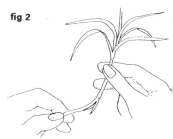

fig 2

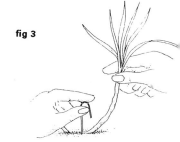

fig 3

fig 4a

fig 4b

HARVESTING

DRYING FLOWERS

Drying the flowers you have grown in your own garden and using them in an arrangement for the winter months is one of the most satisfying and rewarding tasks. *Any* flower head or foliage will dry, but not all of them will be an asset in an arrangement. Some shrivel too much to be attractive and others lose too much of their colour. It is interesting to see how many different flowers you can harvest and which of them will survive well enough to use.

Everlasting flowers

These are the true 'ready-dried' flowers which produce papery, straw-like petals. They don't drop these petals and if they are picked at the correct stage in their development in the summer – though not necessarily in any specific month – they will last for years. They don't fade in sunlight as many other air-dried flowers do.

After planting these annual everlastings in early spring (see page 42) some will be ready for harvesting this month. It is essential to cut everlasting flowers as soon as they reach their prime, or even marginally before. If they are picked too early, the flower head will be closed and the stem will become limp; if cut too late, although the stem will be nicely dried, the flower head will become overblown and brittle and in time will disintegrate.

Cutting the everlastings

This is a continuous process from now until flowering finishes in the autumn.

■ Gather the flowers on a dry day and tie them in small bunches with the heads at different heights, so that they do not crush.
■ Hang them upside down in a cool, airy place such as a garage, loft or shed. Suspending them from a coathanger makes more space.

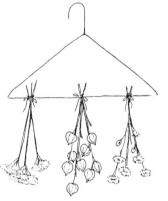

Most varieties of everlastings are useful in flower arranging, although by their nature, they are stiff and the stems of most types are fairly short. Artificial stems from other plants can be wired to a short stem to lengthen it and the new stem then wrapped in florists' tape to conceal the join. Mix the size of flower heads and shape as much as possible in a flower arrangement.

Drying other flowers

These, and other annual flowers you attempt to dry, give the best results if they dry off *slowly*. As long as the stems remain firm they shrivel less than if they are hung up in bunches to air dry.

■ Stand the stem ends in soaked floral foam and allow them to dry naturally, keeping the water topped up. Larkspur and delphiniums, particularly, give much better results this way. Florist's roses can be dried in a similar way.

■ Leave them in the water (or in the arrangement) until the heads begin to flop, then hang them upside down in bunches to finish drying, when the heads will straighten. Most garden roses lose their petals once they die and these are better dried in the microwave, with excellent results (see page 100).

ANNUAL EVERLASTINGS FOR FLOWER ARRANGING

Ammobium alatum – long stems, silvery white petals 2.5cm (1in) across
Celosia 'Pink flamingo' – spikes of two-tone flower heads in pink shading to white
Craspedia globosa – yellow drumsticks
Gomphrena globosa – purple, red, pink and white
Helichrysum bracteatum (Straw flower, mixed colours) – pick single heads only early in the year to allow the other flower buds to develop, add stems of florist's wire, (figs 7,9a&b)
Helipterum humboldianum – golden clusters of tiny flowers
H. manglesii – pinks and white with yellow centres
H. roseum syn. **acrolinium** – larger flowers than *H. manglesii*
Limonium suworowii Statice 'Pink pokers' pink flowering spikes
Molucella – olive green bells which also absorb glycerine well
Xerantheum – wiry stemmed, double crested flower heads in rose, purple, white and lilac

OTHER FLOWERS FOR DRYING

Achillea
Amaranthus (Love-lies-bleeding)
Centaurea macrocephala (golden knapweed)
Delphinium (Larkspur)
Gypsophila (Baby's breath)
Lavender
Solidago (Golden rod)
Zinnia

plants
OF THE
month

NARROW SPEARS
Phormium leaves can be split by tearing them down the length to give spears of different widths for arranging. The tip of the spear can also be shaped to a point, if necessary, with scissors.

SWEET PEA
Lathyrus odoratus

If the rose is everyone's favourite flower, the sweet pea must be a close second. It has the appeal and fragility of a wild rose. Each year new varieties are included in the catalogues, adding new colours, longer stems, wavier petals, more vigorous growth – yet none of this detracts from the delicacy of the flower itself.

Although invaluable for the flower arranger, sweet peas do not suit contrived displays. They need very little arranging – a bowl of mixed or single colours of sweet peas with a very little asparagus fern or silvery grey wormwood *(Artemesia arborescens)* to soften the hard edge of the bowl is all that is needed. The delicate wavy heads also add a softness to mixed flower arrangements.

type	Moderately fast-growing, climbing annual, with tendrils
flowers	Wonderful mixed colours, from midsummer to early autumn
foliage	Single pairs of smooth, ovate, mid-green leaves. Little use except to combine with the flowers themselves
height	Over 2m (6ft)
planting	Sow seeds in late winter under glass, harden off and plant outdoors in late spring. Sow seeds in open ground in early spring
position	Sunny, sheltered. Framework or wall is needed
soil	Deeply dug, fertile soil
care	Feed regularly, but only when buds have formed, for a succession of flowers
propagation	By seed in autumn, protecting over winter, or in spring
varieties for flower arranging	Refer to sweet pea specialist growers' catalogues. 'Charlie's Angel' (blue) 'Champagne Bubbles' (golden amber); 'Queen Mother' (salmon); 'Vera Lynn' (rose); 'Royal Wedding' (white); 'Daphne' (clear lavender); 'Rosalind' (pink)

NEW ZEALAND FLAX
Phormium tenax 'Variegatum'

Indispensable for the flower arranger, the tall sword-shaped leaves are used to give a strong upward line, or they can be torn down the length into thinner strips to give curving, arching lines.

type	Evergreen perennial
flowers	Panicles of dull red, ugly flowers on 1m (3ft) long stems
foliage	Leathery, strap-shaped leaves, striped with green and yellow
height	Up to 2m (6ft)
planting	in mid- or late spring
position	Full sun
soil	Deep, moist, but well-drained soil
care	Remove dead flower stems in the autumn
propagation	By division in spring
varieties for flower arranging	*P. t.* 'Purpureum' has reddish purple coppery leaves; Mountain flax (*P. cookianum* 'Tricolor') has red-, yellow- and green-striped leaves

care	Stake individual flowers or use mesh frames to grow them through, before spikes appear
propagation	By seed. Established plants by division in autumn
varieties for flower arranging	Pacific hybrids have white, pink, purple or blue flowers; belladonna varieties are more loosely branched and delicate

HONEYSUCKLE
Lonicera × tellmanniana

This honeysuckle has no scent but is a strong climbing plant with beautiful, long-lasting foliage that is useful for cutting for most of the summer, even after the plant has finished flowering.

type	Deciduous, fast-growing climber
flowers	Clusters of coppery yellow flowers in summer
foliage	Dark green leaves on graceful twining branches
height	Up to 5m (16ft)
planting	During a mild spell, in early winter to early spring
position	Sun or shade
soil	Fertile, well-drained soil
care	Prune after flowering if necessary
propagation	By semi-hardwood cuttings in late summer or by layering
varieties for flower arranging	*L.* x *americana* is a vigorous, free-flowering honeysuckle with purple-red buds opening to pale yellow. It is very fragrant

DELPHINIUM
Delphinium 'Southern Noblemen'

Most flower arrangers grow the annual larkspur for both cutting and drying, but try growing some of the newer hybrid delphiniums. The range of colours makes a wonderful dried arrangement with little need to add much else, other than perhaps some glycerined foliage. Large-flowered hybrid delphiniums are fun to grow, and the stems will cut into sections when dried to make smaller arrangements.

type	Hardy perennial
flowers	Tall spikes of irregularly cup-shaped, spurred, double florets, closely packed along strong stems. Colours range from white, pale pink, deep pink, burgundy red and blue to bi-colour and purple
foliage	Deeply divided, coarse mid-green leaves
height	1.2–1.5m (4–5ft)
planting	Sow seed in early spring for flowering from midsummer onwards
position	Full sun, with shelter of a wall or trellis
soil	Fertile, rich, well-drained soil

practical project *1*

'SUMMER MELODY'

This arrangement is a loose and informal display of the flowers of high summer. The colours are gentle and the outline and foliage shapes are softly blurred and undefined.

The design is a deliberate attempt to express the warm relaxing days of summer while still producing an eyecatching display.

MATERIALS

The container
A large trug basket

Foliage
Honeysuckle *(Lonicera × tellmanniana)*

Flowers
Roses
Sweet Peas

YOU WILL NEED

a large shallow plastic box
large block of oasis
soft green wire
oasis tape

▪ Fix the plastic container firmly inside the basket by drilling holes in the two sides and inserting wire through these holes and through the base of the basket. Secure the ends underneath the basket. Wedge soaked oasis in the box and secure with oasis tape (fig 1a).

▪ Insert trails of honeysuckle to the back and sides of the basket forming a low triangular shape. Bring trails of honeysuckle over the front edge. Add long-stemmed sweet peas, following this outline (fig 1b).

▪ Fill in with garden roses. Keep the largest and full-blown roses to the front and centre of the design (fig 1c).

NOTE

■ *Baskets go well with any flowers but especially well with country flowers of simple charm such as daisies, sweet peas and old roses. When arranging flowers in a basket, leave the handles showing and allow the flowers to trail over the edges. I admit to being over-enthusiastic with this arrangement and only a very little of the handle is still visible!* ■

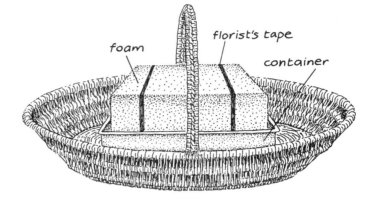

foam   florist's tape   container

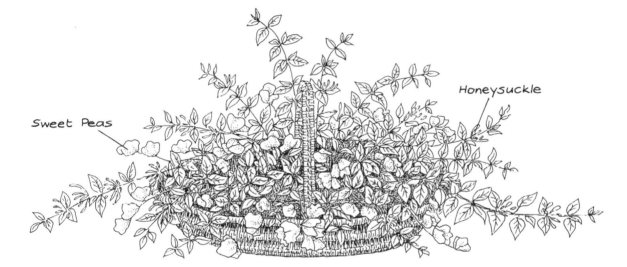

Sweet Peas   Honeysuckle

Roses

practical
project
2

'A RUBY WEDDING'

YOU WILL NEED

2 large blocks of oasis
oasis tape
soft chicken wire
a large, shallow, round,
flat-bottomed bowl

This formal display of roses and lilies on a somewhat original and dominant container is a complete contrast to the soft colours and blurred outline of the arrangement of roses in the trug basket. It was intended for a ruby wedding party, and is bold and symmetrical.

MATERIALS

The container
A pottery elephant, Indian in origin, but now quite common in this country. Any large raised container will do – a pedestal or large raised urn or footed container all suit this type of formal arrangement.

Foliage
Variegated New Zealand flax *(Phormium)*
Ivy *(Hedera colchica* 'Dentata Variegata')
Fern

Flowers
Lilies *(Lilium* 'Star Gazer')
Red roses (to pick up the colours of the lilies)
Copper-coloured roses
Trailing geranium (foliage and flower heads)

■ Lay one block of well-soaked foam on its side in a shallow dish and place the other vertically and to the back. (This shallow dish is the terracotta saucer used under a very large flower pot.) Place crumpled chicken wire over the foam and secure it with florist's tape (fig 2a).

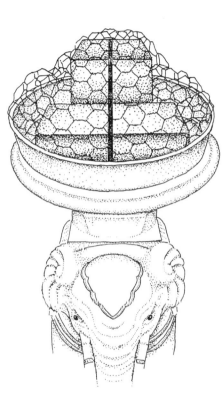

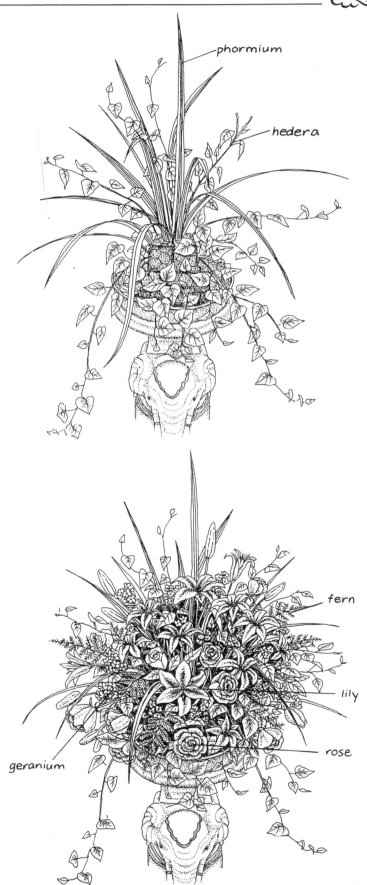

■ Place a central tall blade of New Zealand flax in the centre of the vertical block of foam. Make a triangular outline with New Zealand flax, splitting leaves through the centre so that these thinner leaves curve gracefully to the sides and front. Add long sprays of ivy interspersed between the New Zealand flax, allowing some to trail over the front edge of the dish and to the sides. The trails to each side should be of unequal length (fig 2b).

■ Add the lilies, following the triangular shape, shortening those lower down in the arrangement. To make better use of lilies, thin out some from the cluster of heads to display singly. Nip off the stalk where it joins the main stem. Lengthen the stem by inserting a cigar tube filled with water into the oasis to hold the individual head.

■ Fill in with roses and trails of geranium. Add a few ferns to the centre and sides to soften the outline (fig 2c).

plants
OF THE
month

LILIUM CANDIDUM
The spectacular Madonna lily does not follow the general rules for growing lilies. It is the best known example of a basal rooting lily, it thrives in full sun, against a house wall is ideal, it needs shallow planting in autumn and does well in ordinary, slightly alkaline soil. It grows during the winter, producing rosettes of leaves from the base, followed by fragrant white flowers, with stamens loaded with glistening yellow pollen in early summer (See also page 119).

LILY
Species and hybrids

Lilies have an important place in flower arranging as they can lift a floral display from the commonplace to the regal. There are around 80 species of lily and an ever-increasing number of superb hybrids which are classified by the Royal Horticultural Society into nine divisions.

Two favourite and distinct types which are useful for the flower arranger are those from the Martagon hybrids division (the Turk's Cap type) and the Trumpet and Aurelian hybrids, that is lilies derived chiefly from L. aurelianense.

CULTIVATION
of lilies

With one notable exception – the old Madonna lily (see margin note) – lilies are summer flowering bulbs, dormant in winter. As with all bulbs, lilies need to be given sufficient moisture during the growing and flowering period, but the soil should be well drained. They like well-manured soil and a top dressing of leaf mould during the autumn. If you grow them, as I do, in sandy soil, it helps to dig in well-rotted cow manure at the base of each planting hole.

Most lilies (again, the Madonna lily is an exception), prefer neutral or slightly acid soil. If you have alkaline soil, grow lilies in pots, giving them shelter over the winter to prevent waterlogged icy conditions. Large containers

are needed to give the bulbs the necessary depth for planting.

It is important to determine whether the lily bulb is basal rooting (producing thick roots from the basal plate) or stem rooting (producing extra feeding roots from just above the bulb). Stem rooting bulbs must be planted deeply, at about two and a half times the depth of the bulb and can be planted in either autumn or spring in enriched, fertile soil. Basal rooting bulbs need a thinner covering of soil, about 5cm (2ins) and do best when planted in autumn.

OLYMPIC HYBRIDS
Lilium

This is a vigorous strain of hybrid lilies, which will tolerate lime and produce waxy, almost sculptured looking, long lasting cut flowers.

type	Summer flowering, hardy bulb, stem rooting
flowers	Fragrant, outward facing, trumpet-shaped flowers, up to 20cm across (8in) when well grown. White, tinged with shades of pink with greenish yellow throats. Variants of other shades
foliage	Mid-green, lanceolate
height	1.2–2m (4–6ft)
planting	Plant deeply in autumn or spring
site	Full sun or semi-shade, ideal for patio pots
soil	Fertile, enriched
care	Pinkish tones fade in full sun
propagation	By scales (see page 87)
varieties for flower arranging	The choice is vast. Get a bulb catalogue from a specialist nursery and you will find a colour range to enhance any flower display. Use the space in the garden for more unusual colours, not readily available in the shops.

MARTAGON OR TURK'S CAP LILY
Lilium martagon

If you haven't grown lilies for flower arranging before, this easy subject is a good choice to start your collection. Many attractive and vigorous Martagon hybrids are available.

type	Hardy bulb, basal rooting
flowers	Racemes of pendant, deep rose-coloured flowers with darker spots, turban shaped, that is, recurved and rolled.

	Vigorous grower, producing masses of heads per stem
foliage	Lance shaped, arranged in whorls up the stem
height	1.5m (5ft)
planting	Autumn
site	Semi-shade
soil	Tolerant of any soil
care	Does not like disturbance. Feed during the flowering period
propagation	Will naturalise by self seeding
varieties for flower arranging	*L. martagon album* – pure white flowers
	'Backhouse hybrids' – varying in colour from gold to cream, spotted inside with brownish purple

ASTILBE

Astilbe 'Bressingham Beauty'

Astilbes are a boon to flower arrangers because of their shape. If an arrangement seems too flat or one-dimensional, add some plumes of astilbe and their feathery points will transform it.

type	Clump-forming perennial
flowers	Tiny clear pink flowers in feathery, pyramidal panicles in summer
foliage	Fern-like, deep green foliage, bronze tints to new growth
height	60–90cm (2–3ft)
planting	Mid autumn to early spring
site	Full sun to light shade
soil	Moist, fertile
care	Water during hot dry weather. Mulch as necessary
propagation	By division in spring
varieties	*A.* 'Deutschland' is white

LADY'S MANTLE

Alchemilla mollis

This is a delightful plant to add to any flower arrangement – both flowers and foliage are invaluable for their decorative effect. It is a 'must'.

type	Clump-forming groundcover, perennial
flowers	Sprays of tiny lime-green flowers, with yellow-green calyces in summer
foliage	Hairy, palmate, light green, leaves with serrated edges
height	Up to 50cm (20in)
planting	Autumn or spring
site	Thrives in most areas, but does best in full sun
soil	Well-drained
care	Cut stems almost to the ground after flowering
propagation	Seed, or by division in spring or autumn
varieties for flower arranging	*Alchemilla conjuncta* has very pretty star-shaped leaves with flowers, a miniature replica of *A. mollis*

PINK

Dianthus 'Doris'

Dianthus flowers are usually added to an arrangement and seldom used as a display on their own. A simple but effective arrangement is made by putting the pink 'Doris' in a pewter container with a few fronds of *Artemesia* 'Powis Castle'. The heady scent of pinks is evocative of cottage gardens and childhood.

type	Evergreen, clump forming perennial
flowers	Scented, repeat-flowering, double, pale salmon-pink blooms with darker pink centres
foliage	Cushions of narrow lanceolate grey-green leaves
height	30–45cm (12–18in)
planting	Spring or autumn
site	Full sun
soil	Ordinary light, alkaline soil
care	Stop young pinks, to encourage bushy plants
propagation	Semi-ripe cuttings or by layering
varieties for flower arranging	*Dianthus* 'Daphne' has single, pink flowers each with a red eye; *Dianthus* 'Diane' has double, rosy pink flowers

LILIES FOR FLOWER ARRANGING

'Connecticut King' – yellow

'Enchantment' – rich nasturtium-red

'Star Gazer' – white-edged, pink spotted crimson

L.* × *testaceum (syn. excelsum), apricot-yellow with scarlet anthers

'Green Dragon' – white inside with the outside striped greenish-brown

'Cote d'Azur' – delicate pink

'Corsage' – pale pink, cream centres with maroon spots. Has no pollen

'African Queen' – glowing tangerine flowers with the backs of the petals marked in reddish-brown

'Casa Blanca' – pure white

'Black Dragon' – white trumpets with purplish-brown margins on the outside of the petals

'Green Magic' – pale lemon yellow, flushed with green

Lilium regale (Regal lily) – wine coloured buds opening to silk white interiors with gold throats and stamens

***L. regale* 'Royal Gold'** – pale gold form with a wonderful scent

AUGUST

For the gardener, this time of year evokes the image of the deckchair, the straw hat and the drone of bees – for the flower gardener-and-arranger it is a wonderful month. It is also the busiest time of the year. In no other month is there such an abundance of flowers for picking – summer annuals and perennials, roses, sweet peas, pinks and border carnations, lilies, gladioli and dahlias – all favourites.

But it is the delicate charm of the annuals such as cosmos and lavatera with their fragile petals, as well as the glorious variety of foliage plants and shrubs that makes flower arranging such a joy this month. The harvesting and drying of flowers and foliage continues throughout the month so that we can enjoy them during the winter.

Make the most of dry spells for picking, while they are in peak condition and before stormy weather sets in. Preserve different types of foliage to arrange with them as well, using either desiccant and a microwave or glycerine.

And then there is the task of propagation. Not just the taking of a few cuttings – seeds of perennials and some hardy annuals for next year's flowers can be sown, shrubs layered and some herbaceous plants will be ready for cutting down and division. The end of this month is the time to take cuttings of roses.

Then we begin the forward planning again. What improvements can we make next year? Shall we move that shrub before it gets much older? All the planning that goes on inside the head is the reason why gardeners cannot relax in the garden chairs quite as easily as those whose heart is not in it. We sit and devise new schemes and mentally re-order most of the borders. There is an unquenchable, optimistic streak in every gardener and a strongly acquisitive streak in every flower arranger and both make this a very productive month.

tasks
FOR THE
month

CHECKLIST

☐ Take semi-ripe cuttings, heel cuttings and root cuttings of shrubs and roses

☐ Order lilies from specialist nurseries now

☐ Propagate lilies by taking bulbils or scales

☐ Plan your garden for colours and seasons

PROPAGATION

Propagation simply means increasing the number of your plants. This is done by seed (see p21 and 51) or by vegetative propagation – layering (see p118), division (see p108) or, this month, most successfully by cuttings. A *cutting* is a portion of growth severed from a plant. It is then treated in such a way that it becomes a replica of its parent plant.

fig 1

TYPES OF CUTTING

Hardwood – taken from fully matured wood of deciduous shrubs when the leaves have fallen from mid-autumn onwards (see p118). Hardwood cuttings from evergreen shrubs are more successful when taken in spring.

Softwood – taken from young shoots in spring. They need care and root more readily in a propagating frame (see p29).

Semi-ripe – (sometimes referred to as semi-hardwood or semi-tender summer cuttings) are less mature than hardwood, but firmer than softwood. Taken in summer, they are the easiest and most successful cuttings.

Heel – a semi-ripe or hardwood cutting taken from the parent plant with a heel attached.

Leaf – a cutting taken from a mature leaf.

Root – a cutting taken from a section of root.

There is sufficient growth on shrubs and shrubby foliage plants to provide good semi-hardwood cuttings that will root easily at this time of year.

Semi-ripe cuttings

For a cutting to root (or strike) it must have light, warmth and moisture and a good planting medium. Excellent proprietary brands of seed-and-cuttings compost are available. Alternatively, root cuttings in soil containing (by volume) equal parts of peat and sand. It also helps to buy a hormone rooting powder containing a fungicide to prevent rotting.

▪ Pull a firm but not woody shoot, about 10cm (4in) long, from the parent plant.

▪ Trim the shoot to just below a leaf joint, using a sharp knife to give a clean slanting cut.

▪ Pinch out the soft tip of the cutting which will otherwise wilt, just above a leaf joint, and remove a few lower leaves (fig 1).

▪ Dip the end of the cutting into the rooting powder and shake off the excess.

▪ Using a dibber, gently insert it into a pot of dampened compost to about one third of its length.

▪ Place in a propagating frame, *or* bend two florist's wires at right angles to each other and push them into the

compost to support a clear plastic bag (fig 2).

▪ Keep the pot in a warm place, about 18°C (64°F), out of direct sunshine.

The time taken to root varies according to the type of shrub, from 10 days to three weeks. Once rooted, remove the covering and grow on into larger pots and potting compost. Keep in a cold frame over winter and plant out in spring, once the danger of frost has passed.

Heel cuttings

At this time of year most shrubs will root easily using this method.

▪ Pull the semi-ripe cutting from the main stem with a strip of the bark attached (fig 3).

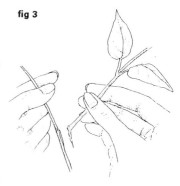

fig 3

▪ Trim the ragged portion neatly with a sharp knife and follow the directions for semi-ripe cuttings above, or for a hardwood cutting.

Roses can also be propagated by cuttings – they can be taken as semi-ripe cuttings now or as hardwood cuttings later in the year. Both give good results. Choose firm, non-flowering side shoots, 23–30cm (9–12in) long. Cut just below a leaf joint at the base of the shoot. Treat as appropriate for the time of year.

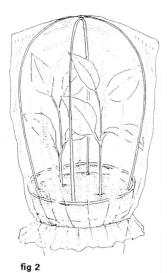

fig 2

Root cuttings

Cuttings can be taken from any part of a plant that contains some cells which have the ability to divide and grow. It is quite possible to take cuttings from the root of a plant, although it is not as popular a method as taking soft- or hardwood cuttings. It is, however, quite a useful thing to know – if you do not catch the seed of the splendid Oriental poppies at the correct time, for example, they will root easily from this type of cutting. So do roses, bear's breeches, bleeding heart, romneya, rudbeckia, mullein and any plant with fleshy roots.

> **NOTE**
>
> ■ *Propagation by root cuttings is not a method that should be used for grafted plants* ■

The best time to take root cuttings is late autumn or winter, when the plants are dormant, or from lifted plants.

■ Scrape the soil away from the plant at one side to expose the root.
■ Cut off a large root cleanly with a knife. Cut it into short lengths about 5cm (2in) long. Make a slanting cut at the base of each cutting and a straight cut at the top (fig 4).
■ Insert the root sections into a pot of cuttings compost, making sure they are the correct way up. The tops of the cuttings should be just below the surface of the compost (fig 5).
■ Keep in a cold frame or in a sheltered area in the open ground over winter.
■ Once growth is well established, feed with liquid fertiliser and pot on individually.

LILIES

Species-type lilies, such as the flower arranger's favourite, the tall-growing Madonna lily *(Lilium candidum)*, and Turk's-cap lilies should be ordered from specialist bulb nurseries this month, for planting in autumn (see page 82).

Propagation by bulbils

The summer-flowering species of lily – tiger lilies, some hybrids and the madonna lily – can be propagated by stem bulbils. These are the tiny, swollen, purplish-green bulbs that appear in the leaf axils. Do not confuse them with bulblets – offsets produced underground (fig 6).

■ Gently ease off the bulbils when they are ripe – that is, when they come away from the stem very easily and the foliage is starting to yellow and die.
■ Plant 1cm (½in) deep in a deep seed tray or flower pots filled with moist John Innes potting compost.
■ Grow on, either in a garden frame or a very sheltered position outdoors, for 2–3 years when they can be planted into their permanent positions to flower. Fertile soil and frequent liquid feeding will encourage the bulbs to flower more readily.

Propagation by scales

The lily bulb is, like other bulbs, made up of overlapping scales, but with one difference: lily scales can easily be detached from the bulb and used for propagation. This can be undertaken at any time of year when the bulb is out of the ground, either when dug up for transplanting or when the lilies are first bought. For older bulbs, first remove and discard any very old, unhealthy scales from the outside.

■ Gently tease off a fleshy, healthy scale, so that it parts from the main bulb at the roots (fig 7). Allow at least three quarters of the bulb to remain intact, or it will not flower that year.
■ Dust the individual scales with a fungicide to help prevent mould.
■ Fill a deep seed tray or flower pots with lightly moistened potting compost and bury two thirds of the scale, pointed end uppermost (fig 8). Keep them in a warm place 21°C (70°F). Tiny bulbs then begin to develop at the base of the scales.
■ Grow on as for bulbils. It will normally take several years before lily bulbs propagated from scales produce flowers.

PLANNING

USING COLOUR

More than in any other month there now is a riot of colour in the garden. It is a good time to look around the garden, at colour combinations that please you, and to make a note to alter any that do not.

There is a great deal to be gained at this time of year by going round gardens that are open to the public, enjoying other people's planting schemes and appreciating their colour combinations. Although you will get many ideas for your own garden, in the end you are growing plants for the colour schemes of the rooms you decorate with flowers. In the garden itself, give some thought to the way the plants blend into the overall colour scheme of the garden – and plant what gives *you* pleasure. To help you with your planning the chart on pages 139–141 shows the colour and flowering season of just a few of the many plants which can be used.

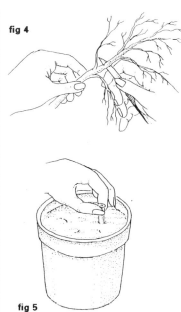

fig 4

fig 5

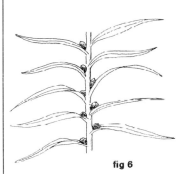

fig 6

fig 7

fig 8

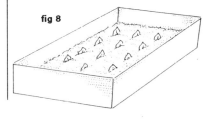

plants

OF THE

month

CLEMATIS
Clematis

There are over 250 species of clematis and, in general, the most commonly grown are the least interesting. The popular spring and mid-season flowering varieties are very useful to the flower arranger, and trails of *any* clematis foliage are wonderful for pedestal arrangements. But take a close look at some of the later-flowering hybrid varieties in the catalogues. There are some choice small-flowered cultivars, flowering in autumn. My own favourite has to be *Clematis tangutica*.

type	Deciduous climber
flowers	There is great variation in shape, size and colour of flowers
foliage	Trails of clematis foliage are invaluable for pedestal arrangements
height	Up to 6m (20ft)
planting	In mid-autumn to late spring
position	Sunny, with roots in the shade. A flower bed on a paved patio against a wall is ideal
soil	Alkaline soil
care	Mulch in spring. Prune dead wood and shorten if necessary to restrict growth. Tie in young shoots
propagation	By semi-ripe stem cuttings with 2–3 buds in midsummer
varieties for flower arranging	*C. tangutica* has buttercup-yellow, lantern-shaped flowers in late summer to mid-autumn. Very attractive fluffy silver seed heads last all winter in a sheltered site. *C. orientalis* has yellow, mildly scented, star-shaped flowers in late summer to mid-autumn and small silver-grey seed heads

COSMOS
Cosmos bipinnatus

With their 'country garden' charm, these make the flower arranger's task very easy. Add the delicate open faces of cosmos to any arrangement and it will lose its stiffness or formality. They are now available in many delightful shades, including chocolate.

type	Half-hardy annual
flowers	Daisy type, in shades of pink and white, midsummer onwards
foliage	Graceful, fernlike
height	30–100cm (12–36in)
planting	In late spring
position	Full sun
soil	Light, poor soil. Rich soil produces foliage at the expense of flowers
care	Deadhead for continued flowering. May need to be staked
propagation	Sow seed under glass in late winter and early spring
varieties for flower arranging	*C. b.* 'Sensation Mixed' is an early, large-flowering strain in red, pink and white; *C. b.* 'Daydream' has semi-dwarf, very pale pink flowers with deep pink centres; *C. b.* 'Sulphureos Sunset' has orange, semi-double flowers

ANNUAL MALLOW
Lavatera trimestris 'Pink Beauty'

One of the most rewarding annuals to grow, and this variety is one I never miss. It flowers profusely from midsummer until mid-autumn.

type	Half-hardy annual
flowers	Glistening, trumpet-like in a soft pink, veined with deep rose, midsummer to mid-autumn
foliage	Heart-shaped, bright green, not very useful
height	90cm (3ft)
planting	Sow seed under glass in late winter or directly into open ground in late spring
position	Full sun, sheltered from wind
soil	Any soil
care	Feed lightly with proprietary flower fertiliser, once flower buds appear
propagation	By seed
varieties for flower arranging	*L. t.* 'Silver Cup' is a slightly deeper pink than 'Pink Beauty'; *L. t.* 'Mont Blanc' has white flowers and light green foliage. It grows to 50cm (20in)

COMMON BEECH
Fagus sylvatica

This has one of the most versatile foliages for the flower arranger. The soft spring-green and the darker mid-season beech leaves are wonderful as a background for any arrangement. From midsummer onwards, long sprays of beech can be preserved in glycerine to add to winter displays of fresh or dried flowers.

type	Deciduous tree
flowers	Insignificant
foliage	Alternate, ovate, wavy-edged leaves that turn copper in the autumn. Graceful stems
height	Can be trimmed as a hedge. As a tree it will reach 20m (70ft)
planting	In autumn to spring
position	Sun or semi-shade
soil	Any well-drained soil
care	To grow as a hedge, remove the upper quarter of all shoots after planting. Tip shoots frequently to make a thick hedge
propagation	By seed in autumn, usually a job for the nurseryman
varieties for flower arranging	Copper beech (F. *purpurea*) has rich copper foliage

BABY'S BREATH
Gypsophila paniculata

This plant can be difficult to establish, but once settled can be left undisturbed for years. It is useful to the flower arranger but more popular with florists. It gives a softness to a formal display. Don't be tempted to use too much in an arrangement – it may spoil the outline.

type	Deciduous perennial
flowers	Tiny, double, white, round, in spreading panicles on wiry branching stems
foliage	Linear and insignificant, at base of stems
height	60–90cm (24–36in)
planting	In spring
position	Full sun
soil	Alkaline, fertile, well-drained soil
care	Trim after first flowers to encourage succession
propagation	By softwood cuttings in early summer or by seed under glass in early spring
varieties for flower arranging	*G.p.* 'Flamingo' has double pink flowers. It is a short-lived perennial; 'Bristol Fairy' has double white flowers

practical project *1*

'A GENTLE WELCOME'

This flower arrangement was created for a bed-side table for a guest. The soft pink of the roses is restful and blends with the room decoration to give a gentle welcome to emphasise the restful atmosphere of the room.

MATERIALS

The container
A double candle holder made from attractively twisted wire on a metal base and sprayed gold. One candle holder holds the candle it was designed for. The other is adapted to hold flowers by the addition of a candle cup (see p32). The floral foam is wedged into the cup and secured with tape (fig 1a). A second small container and oasis is placed at the foot of the candlestick.

Foliage
Ivy (*Hedera helix* 'Glacier')
Asparagus fern

Flowers
Clematis tangutica
Campanula isophylla 'Alba'
Rosa 'New Dawn'
Baby's Breath (*Gypsophila paniculata*)

YOU WILL NEED
floral foam
florist's tape
oasis

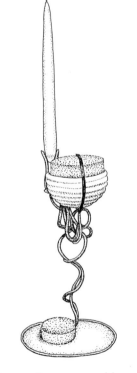

■ Place the candle to start with to get the balance between the height and the amount of flowers and foliage used. (The finished display must not be visually unbalanced or appear top-heavy.)
■ Insert short stems of ivy and asparagus fern into both containers. Allow some stems to trail downwards, to the right side, from the top cup (fig 1b).
■ Add very short sprigs of clematis and campanula at top and bottom.
■ Add the roses, with the larger blooms to the centre and small buds to the outside.
■ Finally, add a very few light sprigs of baby's breath towards the centre of each cup (fig 1c).

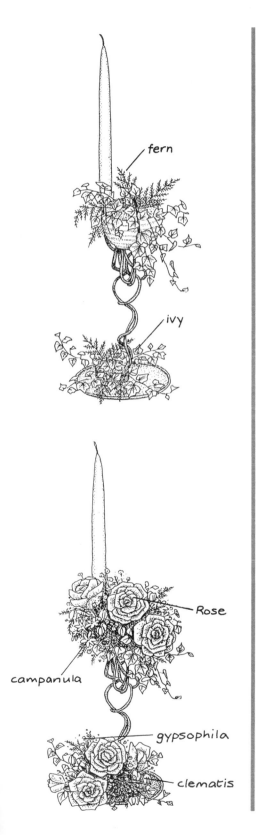

fern

ivy

Rose

campanula

gypsophila

clematis

practical project *2*

'HIGH SUMMER'

YOU WILL NEED

a large block of oasis foam
see picture page 85

A pot brimming with garden annuals is one of the joys of this month. It is also one of the easiest arrangements to make, providing you have the right type of pot. A bowl (that is, a container with the top wider than the base), will hold a wonderful selection of annuals, but it will not show them off to the same advantage. A bowl gives the impression that the stems have been cut off. The water pot shape doesn't do this and it helps the flowers by providing them with a 'stem'. The fact that it is green also helps. Both the balance and proportion of the arrangement are satisfying. The same flowers in a bowl would become more of a 'mass' arrangement and lose its pleasing and rather elegant curving lines.

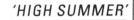

MATERIALS

The container
a water pot

Foliage
Beech *(Fagus)*
Variegated privet
(Ligustrum ovalifolium 'Variegata')
Ballota pseudodictamnus

Flowers
Lavatera 'Pink Beauty'
Snapdragon *(Antirrhinum)*
Rambling rose 'Dorothy Perkins'
Scabious
Cosmos
Lady's mantle *(Alchemilla mollis)*

practical project

2

'HIGH SUMMER'

continued

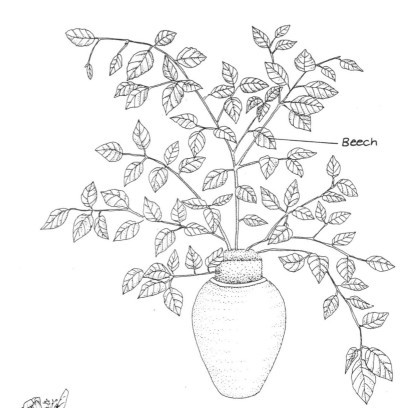

Beech

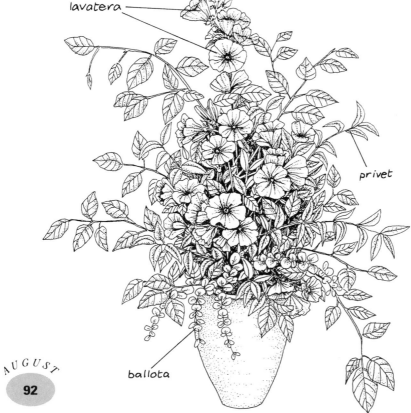

lavatera

privet

ballota

- The oasis must have something to 'sit on' so that it does not fall down into the well of the pot. Fill up the pot with old discarded oasis or crumpled newspaper and wedge the oasis block in the neck of the pot.
- Insert a long spray of beech to about one and a half times the height of the pot, towards the back of the oasis. Trim off extra leaves if it is densely foliated. Add trails to the sides and coming towards the front, forming a loosely triangular outline (fig 2a).

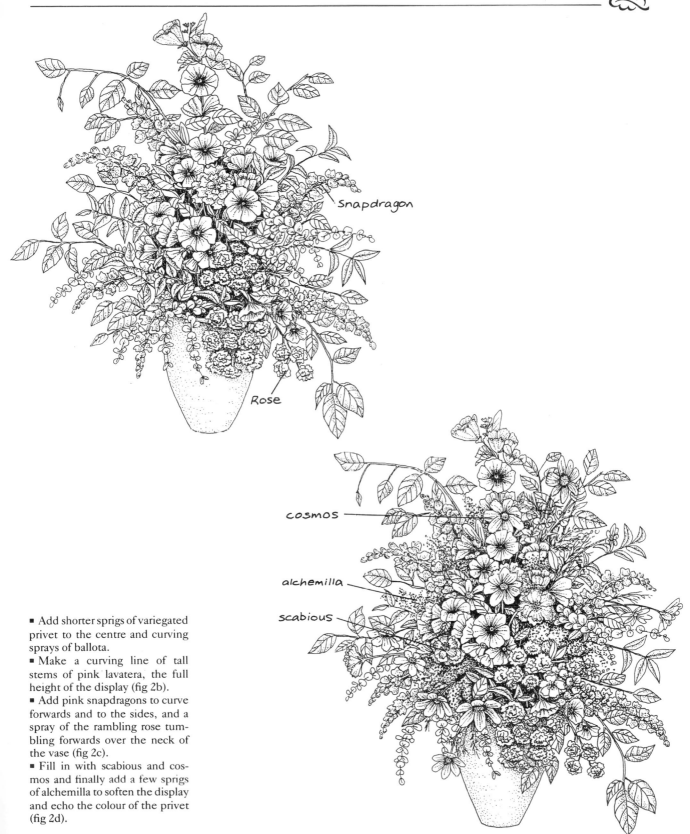

Snapdragon

Rose

cosmos

alchemilla

scabious

■ Add shorter sprigs of variegated privet to the centre and curving sprays of ballota.

■ Make a curving line of tall stems of pink lavatera, the full height of the display (fig 2b).

■ Add pink snapdragons to curve forwards and to the sides, and a spray of the rambling rose tumbling forwards over the neck of the vase (fig 2c).

■ Fill in with scabious and cosmos and finally add a few sprigs of alchemilla to soften the display and echo the colour of the privet (fig 2d).

SEPTEMBER

Early autumn is a golden time of the year — pale sunshine on copper leaves, berries and rose hips spilling from hedgerows, defiant autumn bulbs like nerines and brassy plants like rudbeckias offering consolation for the mound of annuals wilting on the compost heap. Before the leaves crisp and the sap stops rising, it is not too late to preserve foliage with glycerine early in the month.

Beech leaves, treated as they begin to turn colour, go a very attractive copper shade, quite different from the dark greeny brown of beech preserved in midsummer.

This month also always has a melancholy feeling to it. The days are shortening and a nip in the air in the early mornings is a reminder of cold days to come and of plants that need protection. Dahlias and gladioli will need to be lifted before much longer and the ground looks empty and bereft. On the positive side, there are cuttings to take — it is the best month for propagating geraniums and hydrangeas if you can give them protection over the winter. Sweet peas can be planted for the choicest blooms next year and seeds of hardy annuals will overwinter if they are sown out-of-doors this month.

Winter evening community activities take up again this month. There are flower clubs in most areas with regular demonstrations on flower arranging from qualified experts. There are also national and international flower arranging societies and competitions that take the art to a very high level.

tasks
FOR THE
month

AUTUMN COLOUR FOR FLOWER ARRANGING

Abelia* × *grandiflora – Semi-evergreen, with usually some flowers still clinging to the branches even when the foliage is turning its autumn yellow

Acer – in variety, with brilliant autumn shades of red or russet

Amelanchier canadensis – autumn shades of red, yellow and orange

Berberis* × *rubrostilla – red and orange foliage with red pear-shaped berries

***Berberis thunbergii* 'Atropurpurea Nana'** – dark purple foliage in summer, scarlet red with berries in autumn

***Cotinus coggygria* 'Notcutt's Variety'** – Round, grape-purple leaves in summer turning bright red in autumn

Cotoneaster franchetii – autumn foliage not as striking as other shrubs, spectacular berries ignored by birds

Fothergilla major – deep orange and gold autumn leaves, fragrant brush-like white flowers in spring

Parrotia – slow-growing shrub, autumn foliage is amber, red and gold

Sumach *(Rhus typhina)* – contributes to the glories of the Canadian fall. Flame-coloured autumn foliage

Wild spindle tree *(Euonymus europaeus* 'Red Cascade') – autumn foliage soft pink, rose-red seed capsules (poisonous)

CHECKLIST

☐ Sow sweet peas for flowering in the following year
☐ Lift gladioli and store over winter
☐ Start a compost heap
☐ Choose and plant new herbaceous plants
☐ Plant groundcover plants

PROPAGATION

SWEET PEAS

The best sweet peas for flower arranging are, fortunately, not the exhibition-size blooms with straight and sturdy stems. Wonderful though these are, it is the cottage garden charm and the delicacy of their colouring that contribute most as far as the flower arranger is concerned. Twisted curling stems and tendrils and informal blooms make sweet peas a favourite for the flower arranger. Bigger sweet peas will, however, add more to a display and we do want them to flower as early in the year as possible. The bouquet on page 78 was photographed in early summer. The sweet peas in it were sown in open ground in early autumn and began to flower the following year in late spring.

Sowing sweet peas in the open ground

As long as you can give the seeds a warm, sheltered wall as their permanent protection and fertile, well-drained soil, the seed can be sown direct in the open ground this month or next, where they are to flower. A little frost will not harm sweet pea seedlings, but a light covering of bracken or straw is advisable in severe weather conditions. If you cannot provide sheltered conditions for them, sow the seeds individually in pots and overwinter them in a cold frame or cold greenhouse *(see sowing sweet peas p21)*. Transplant into their permanent positions when they are growing strongly, in a mild spell, as the soil is warming up, early in the following year.

MAINTENANCE

GLADIOLI

Large-flowered gladioli will not survive many winters in cooler climates, 'Nanus' varieties in sheltered areas under a wall will (see page 42). The others must be lifted at the end of this month.

■ As the foliage dies down, ease the corms from the ground with a fork. Remove the soil.

■ Cut off all but 2.5cm (1in) of the stem with secateurs. Place the corms in a dry, airy place for a few weeks until absolutely dry.

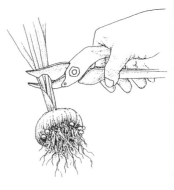

■ Remove any small bulblets, store these as well to grow on. Ease off the old, shrivelled corm at the base.

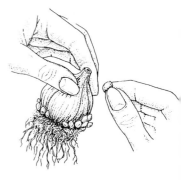

■ Store them in boxes in a dry, frost-proof shed or in a cold room. If the corms are stored in a warm room, they will shrivel.

MAKING A COMPOST HEAP

Composting garden waste and digging it back into the soil to provide humus is the best way to improve your soil and get better plants. Regular applications on clay soils helps to separate the sticky, fine particles of clay and so provide air spaces. This opens up the soil and gives better drainage. The soil also warms up more quickly and eventually becomes far easier to work. On sandy soils, the compost helps to bind the larger particles together – which in turn means that the soil is capable of holding water better. On any type of soil it provides nutrients and improves the overall soil structure.

Choice of containers

The container or compost bin does not have to be expensive. You can spend nothing and merely start a heap in a hidden corner of the garden. The cubic volume of any heap is important as it needs to heat up in the centre, so make it as wide as it is high. Cover it with a plastic sheet, held down by four bricks, once you have finished adding to the heap. A small outlay will buy a slatted, green plastic bin with a lid, from a hardware shop. More expensive, but a very efficient solution, is the slatted timber compost

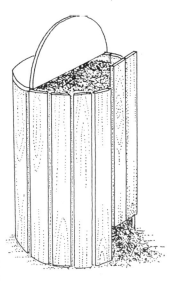

container, sold ready-to-assemble. With a few floor boards and some posts anyone can build a similar one cheaply.

Feeding the compost heap

■ Anything organic – vegetable waste, leaves, flowers, annual weeds, non-woody hedge clippings, tea leaves, egg shells and grass cuttings mixed with bulkier organic matter such as fallen leaves.
■ Spread a 15cm (6in) layer of waste over the base of the container. Water, if dry.
■ Sprinkle a proprietary activator or sulphate of ammonia over the top at a rate of 25g per square metre (about 1oz per square yard).
■ Continue to build up the heap in this way, keeping it moist.
■ When the bin is full, put on the lid, and in six months the compost should be dark, crumbly and ready for use. During the six months the compost can be turned 'sides to middle' once or twice to help even rotting throughout the heap.

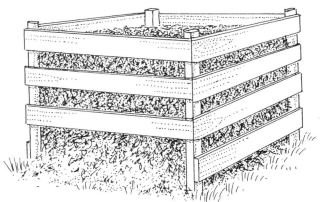

P L A N T I N G

PLANTING GROUNDCOVER

For the flower arranger, trailing groundcover plants can be extremely useful and can be planted this month. Most gardeners choose groundcover for its quick spreading habit and some of the fastest growing groundcover plants such as snow-in-summer *(Cerastium tomentosum)* are of little use in flower arrangement, but others like London pride *(Saxifraga umbrosa)* are useful both for flowers and for the rosettes of their evergreen foliage. Those that produce runners are the most useful of all. These can trail gracefully down in a pedestal arrangement,

softening a hard outline into artistic curves. Others make good groundcover by spreading into a dense mat or clumps.

IVY

Ivy deserves a special mention for flower arranging. Ivies are so common that we almost do not notice them. But when you take up flower arranging, you realise what a valuable and exciting plant the ivy is and how easily it can transform a flower arrangement (see p.104).

HERBACEOUS PLANTS

Choosing and planting new flowers and foliage plants can begin in earnest this month. Most container-grown plants can be planted if the weather is suitable from now until mid-spring. The earlier a plant is put in the better headway it makes the following year.

The same applies to shrubs. Look around at other people's gardens and visit parks and nurseries to discover the number of shrubs that are now aglow with wonderful autumn tints, which make dramatic arrangements although not long lasting.

GROUNDCOVER FOR FLOWER ARRANGING

Another way of discouraging weeds is to make sure that there is no bare earth where self-seeded weeds can settle and germinate. This is achieved by covering the ground with suitable plants – plants that spread, forming dense clumps, or plants that trail, covering the ground with foliage and so exclude the light.

Arum italicum 'Pictum'
Brunnera macrophylla 'Variegata'
Bugle *(Ajuga reptans)*
Elephant's ears *(Bergenia cordifolia)*
B.c. purpurea
Epimedium × rubrum
Euonymus fortunei
Galeobdolon luteum (invasive)
Geranium grandiflorum and
G. pratense 'Johnson's Blue'
Hebe pinguifolia 'Pagei'
Houttuynia cordata
Lamb's ears – lamb's lugs in Scotland! *(Stachys olympica)*
Lamium maculatum (invasive)
Pachysandra terminalis 'Variegata'
Periwinkle *(Vinca major* and *V. minor)*
Polygonum affine 'Dimity' and other varieties
Saxifraga umbrosa
Thyme *(Thymus praecox arcticus)*

plants
OF THE
month

BORDER DAHLIAS
Dahlia

There are many different types of dahlia. Bedding dahlias are grown as annuals from seed but it is the border dahlia which is of interest to the flower arranger. This large group includes singles, collarettes, decoratives with double flowers and broad petals and cactus-type dahlias with narrow, pointed petals, some of which have heads the size of tea plates; pom-pom and ball dahlias with completely round heads and the less commonly grown anemone- and orchid-flowered varieties.

type	Tuberous-rooted, tender perennials
flowers	Extensive colour range with wonderful combinations from midsummer to the first frost
foliage	Coarse, pinnate leaves, not useful for arranging
height	Varies according to variety
planting	Unsprouted tubers in mid-spring, 10cm (4in) deep in sheltered areas and frost-free corners. In other areas, cover tubers with peat under glass or indoors to encourage sprouting
position	Full sun or light shade, sheltered
soil	Fertile, well-cultivated soil
care	Stake tall varieties. Stop plants by pinching out leading shoots once they are growing strongly. Disbud for larger flowers. Lift and store the tubers in the autumn
propagation	By division of tubers (see p.38)
varieties for flower arranging	*Cactus* 'Apple Blossom' (pink); 'Autumn Fire' (orange); 'Athalie' (deep pink); *Decorative* 'Early Bird' (clear yellow); 'Flutterby' (yellow, orange tipped); 'Edinburgh' (purple, white tipped); *Collarette* 'Easter Sunday' (white, yellow centre); 'Clair de Lune' (yellow, gold centre)

LORDS AND LADIES
Arum italicum

The striking and distinctive white-veined leaves appear in late autumn and are still beautiful in mid-winter when foliage is scarce. This plant is very useful in flower arranging because of its sculptural qualities, and a good ground cover once established.

type	Tuberous perennial
flowers	Pale yellowy-green spathes in mid- and late spring. Poisonous red berries in late summer
foliage	Has semi-erect, narrow, white-veined leaves
height	15–25cm (6–10in)
planting	Plant when dormant in late summer to autumn
position	Shade or dappled shade
soil	Moist
care	Keep children away from poisonous berries
propagation	By division in autumn or by separating offsets
varieties for flower arranging	*A. i.* 'Pictum' has cream- or white-veined leaves and red berries in autumn

GUERNSEY LILY
Nerine bowdenii

These are invaluable in the garden because their shocking-pink umbels of flowers appear just when most of the other garden flowers are on their way out. With their strident colour they are difficult to combine with other flowers but should find a corner in the flower arranger's garden.

type	Almost hardy bulb
flowers	Iridescent pink spherical heads of wavy petals, borne in loose umbels on leafless stems 10–12cm (4–5in) across
foliage	Strap-shaped, mid-green, appearing just after the flowers
height	45–60cm (18–24in)
planting	In autumn or spring, 10cm (4in) deep
position	Sunny border, preferably against a wall
soil	Ordinary, well-drained soil
care	Protect with straw or bracken in a severe winter. Nerines do not like disturbance
propagation	By division
varieties for flower arranging	*N. b.* 'Fenwick's Variety' larger flowers; *N. b. alba* has white, pink-flushed flowers; *N. b.* 'Brian Doe' has salmon pink flowers

BERGENIA
Bergenia cordifolia purpurea

This is essential for the flower arranger and also a valuable groundcover plant for the gardener. It is extremely easy to grow, spreads slowly and is evergreen. The stems grow longest in winter, changing colour a little with the seasons. The leaves vary in size according to their age, and so there is always a supply of both large and smaller evergreen leaves for the focal point of an arrangement.

type	Evergreen, spreading perennial
flowers	Racemes of light pink, bell-shaped flowers in spring, not really of great use to the flower arranger as the stems are soft and floppy
foliage	Brown-to-purple-tinged leaves in winter
height	30cm (12in)
planting	In autumn or spring
position	Any site
soil	Tolerates any soil
care	Leave undisturbed, remove flower stems after flowering
propagation	By division in autumn or spring
varieties for flower arranging	*B. cordifolia purpurea* has purple leaves; *B. stracheya* 'Silberlicht' has white flowers and smaller leaves

practical
project
1

MICROWAVED
FLOWERS
AND FOLIAGE

YOU WILL NEED

a quantity of silica gel

FLOWERS TO MICROWAVE

Roses – half-opened, salmon and orange shades are the most successful; '**Glenfiddich**' is superb; some red roses change colour
Cornflower (*Centaurea cyanus*)
Daisy-type flowers
Achillea
Asters
Chrysanthemum frutescens
Double daisies (*Bellis perennis*)
Feverfew
Matricaria
All types of marigolds – especially
French marigold (*Tagetes patula*)
Pinks and carnations (*Dianthus*) – red carnations become purplish in tone

At the beginning of this month the flower garden begins to look straggly. This is the time to rescue dry flower heads and the last of the garden roses and dry them off completely, for use in dried arrangements over the winter. They can be dried in a microwave oven. Not only roses, but many other flowers and foliage dry well this way. The microwaved flower obviously looks slightly more papery than the original, but with patience and a little trial and error you can achieve a flower arrangement that is almost indistinguishable from the real thing.

Silica gel is a desiccant and not in fact a gel at all. It looks like crystals of fine sugar that absorb the moisture from the flower. Most chemists can get silica gel for you, but some silica crystals are too large, and some is now sold with a blue colouring agent that is unsuitable for flower drying. The most satisfactory way to obtain suitable silica gel is to look for proprietary brands in the small ads at the back of a flower arranger's magazine. At the same time, buy a spray to use on the dried flowers to prevent the re-absorption of moisture. Silica gel crystals can be dried off and used for years.

Drying a single rose

■ Pick a half-opened rose on a dry day, leaving a short stem of about 2.5cm (1in).
■ Decant the silica gel into a jug. Pour crystals to a depth of about 2.5cm (1in) into a coffee mug. Stand the rose upright in the silica gel. Very carefully pour silica gel over the rose, starting between the petals and the sides of the mug and pouring crystals gently between the petals so that as far as possible the rose keeps its shape. Completely cover the rose with silica gel.
■ 'Cook' the rose in the microwave for 2 mins 30 seconds. Remove the mug without disturbing the contents and allow to cool completely before gently pouring off the crystals.

Adding a stem

■ Twist a florist's fine green stem wire around the short stem of the rose and stand it upright in a block of unsoaked oasis until you are ready to arrange it.
■ Spray at once with acrylic flower preserving spray if you have it.
■ *Always* keep microwaved flowers in a dry atmosphere.

Drying two or more roses

■ Use a vegetable dish and increase the cooking time. As with most microwave cookery, trial and error is the only way to get perfect results.

Drying foliage

■ Cover the base of a casserole dish with silica gel. Spread single leaves or curving trails of foliage on top.
■ Carefully pour more crystals over the top to cover the foliage completely. Try to keep the undulating shape of the stems as they look more realistic than totally flat foliage. Microwave on full power for 2 minutes. Allow to cool completely in the dish before gently pouring off the crystals. If you need to lengthen the stems for an arrangement, use florist's fine stem wire as for the flowers.

Drying without a microwave

If you do not have a microwave oven you can still dry flowers and foliage in desiccant, it just takes longer. The procedure is exactly the same as above, but it will take three days to a week for most flowers and foliage to dry.

• Carefully ease out one flower after three days to see whether to remove the plants or leave them in a little longer. If they are dry and papery to feel, they are ready.

Arranging microwaved flowers and foliage

The drawback with all desiccant- and microwave-dried flowers is that they are brittle. So a simple arrangement, with all the heads fairly close together to protect each other, is the best way to display them. Keep them on a shelf or anywhere where they will not be brushed against or knocked.

MATERIALS

The container
An oblong trough made from bark with a greenish tone

Foliage
Fern
Ivy (*Hedera helix* 'Glacier')
Ballota pseudodictamus

Flowers
Small to medium-size flowers in good condition – those in the photograph are:
Rosa 'Glenfiddich'
Argyranthemum *(Chrysanthemum frutescens)*
Sweet peas
Achillea 'Cloth of Gold'

• Wedge dry oasis foam in the container, allowing it to extend 2.5cm (1in) higher than the lip of the trough.
• Using wire to extend the stems if necessary, make a framework of fern and ivy, in an asymmetrical triangle to the back and sides of the

AN ARRANGEMENT OF MICROWAVED FLOWERS

YOU WILL NEED

dry oasis foam
florist's wire
acrylic flower spray

FOLIAGE TO MICROWAVE

Astilbes
Eucalyptus – all varieties
Ferns – the smaller varieties
Ivy, all types – in particular silver-edged leaves such as ***Hedera helix*** **'Glacier'** or **'Adam'**; all variegated varieties are good
Rose foliage – in good condition
Spireas

> ### NOTE
> • *If daisy-type flowers flop out of shape, lay them face down on a little silica gel to dry them further. Misshapen petals can be flattened out with the point of a warm iron* •

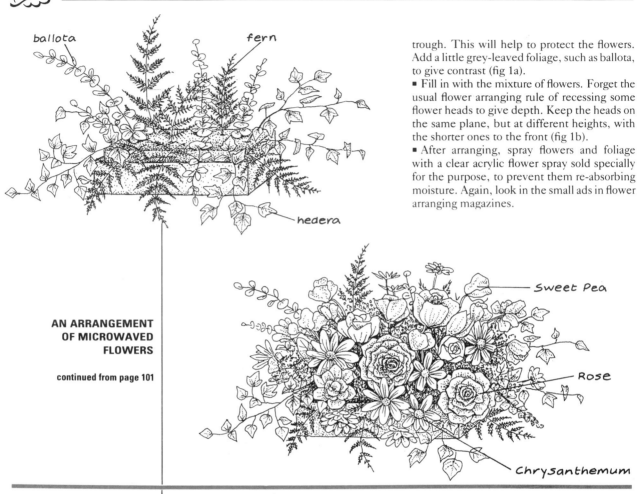

ballota

fern

hedera

Sweet Pea

Rose

Chrysanthemum

trough. This will help to protect the flowers. Add a little grey-leaved foliage, such as ballota, to give contrast (fig 1a).

■ Fill in with the mixture of flowers. Forget the usual flower arranging rule of recessing some flower heads to give depth. Keep the heads on the same plane, but at different heights, with the shorter ones to the front (fig 1b).

■ After arranging, spray flowers and foliage with a clear acrylic flower spray sold specially for the purpose, to prevent them re-absorbing moisture. Again, look in the small ads in flower arranging magazines.

**AN ARRANGEMENT
OF MICROWAVED
FLOWERS**

continued from page 101

practical
project
2

'GLEANINGS FROM
THE GARDEN'

The colour of the autumn foliage makes this a very satisfying month for the flower arranger. In this arrangement the bronze and red shades of the dying *Euphorbia griffithii* 'Fireglow' are echoed in the copper accessories. A few of the last roses and annual snapdragons with the first apples from the orchard strengthen the autumnal feeling.

MATERIALS

The container
a round copper bowl

Foliage
Fuchsia × 'Bacillaris'
Euphorbia
Weigela florida 'Variegata'
Peonia foliage

Flowers
Sedum spectabile
Nerine bowdenii
Pink snapdragons
Dahlias
Rosa 'Queen Elizabeth'

YOU WILL NEED

soaked oasis
copper accessories

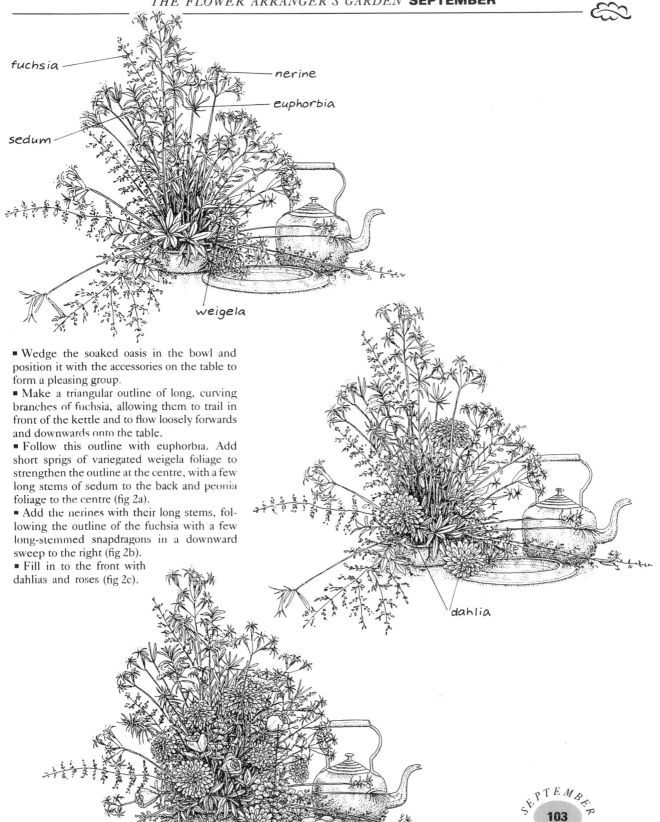

fuchsia

nerine

euphorbia

sedum

weigela

- Wedge the soaked oasis in the bowl and position it with the accessories on the table to form a pleasing group.
- Make a triangular outline of long, curving branches of fuchsia, allowing them to trail in front of the kettle and to flow loosely forwards and downwards onto the table.
- Follow this outline with euphorbia. Add short sprigs of variegated weigela foliage to strengthen the outline at the centre, with a few long stems of sedum to the back and peonia foliage to the centre (fig 2a).
- Add the nerines with their long stems, following the outline of the fuchsia with a few long-stemmed snapdragons in a downward sweep to the right (fig 2b).
- Fill in to the front with dahlias and roses (fig 2c).

dahlia

rose

plants
OF THE
month

HEDERA COLCHICA
The larger leaves of the species
H. colchica are less useful in
flower arranging as they tend to
droop, apart from the variety
H.c. 'Dentata Variegata'. This has
creamy-yellow variegated leaves.
Height 5m (15ft).

IVY
Species and hybrids

Until you begin to arrange flowers, it is easy to overlook the common ivy (Hedera helix) growing in your garden. Once you see the potential of its variegation in colour and the different leaf shapes available, you realise why ivy is the flower arranger's best ally.

Ivy has two distinct forms of growth. The young ivy, which trails and climbs, produces runners with aerial roots and has lobed leaves. The adult ivy, once it has reached the top of a wall or a high tree, produces oval, entire leaves with wavy margins and no aerial roots. It produces flowers and fruits and is known as arborescent ivy.

Single large ivy leaves are often used in groups of three or four, in the centre of a flower arrangement to add depth or to unify smaller, fussy foliages. Single, variegated ivy leaves used in this way lighten an arrangement of dark foliage.

Trails of small ivy leaves are often used to give movement and lightness in an arrangement. Pedestal arrangements rely on trailing branches of ivy and other curving foliages to soften the triangular outline and create a natural, flowing look.

If you are not satisfied with a flower arrangement you have made, try adding variegated ivy. It can alter it completely.

Although the fruits are sometimes useful in Christmas flower arranging, the juvenile forms of ivy are the most useful for arrangers.

	leaves prefer more light and sun
care	Prune in spring to remove damaged stems and restrict growth
propagation	By semi-hardwood cutting in summer, or by layering
varieties for flower arranging	*H.h.* 'Glacier' – Height 3m (10ft) Dainty leaves with variegation of silvery-grey and green
	H.h. 'Goldheart' – Height 6m (20ft), dark green leaves splashed with bright yellow centres
	H.h. 'Eva' – a less rampant ivy, with a spread of only 1m (3ft) and reaching about 1.2m (4ft), dainty grey-green leaves with cream variegation
	H.h. 'Buttercup' – Reaches only 2m (6ft) in height, grown in full sun, the leaves turn the colour of butter
	H.h. 'Atropurpurea' – Height 4m (12ft), dark green leaves which turn purple in winter

COMMON IVY
Hedera helix

The native common ivy is a woodland plant and although growth may be slow for a year or two, once established, the plant will grow more rapidly.

type	Evergreen, woody-stemmed, hardy climber
foliage	Dark green, 5-lobed, invasive. Prettier cultivars are more useful in flower arranging
height	10m (30ft)
spread	5m (15ft)
planting	Between autumn and spring
soil	Any, but as ivies are deep rooted, the soil should be well forked over and well drained
position	Any, but ivies with variegated

CANARY ISLAND IVY
Hedera canariensis

This species is also invaluable in flower arranging, with quite a different leaf form and rather more erect than *H. helix.*

type	Evergreen, self clinging, half hardy climber. A rapid grower, once established
foliage	Leathery, oval to triangular leaves, unlobed, with purplish stems. They are bright green in summer and a bronze-green in winter
height	6m (20ft)
spread	5m (15ft)

planting	Between autumn and spring
soil	Well drained, fertile
position	Thrives against a wall, in a sheltered spot, sun or semi-shade
care	May be damaged in severe winters, cut away affected shoots
propagation	By semi-hardwood cutting in summer, or by layering
varieties for flower arranging	*H.c.* 'Variegata' (syn. 'Gloire de Marengo') – Green leaves with shadings of grey and creamy-white borders. Height and spread as above
	H.c. 'Ravenholst' – A very vigorous, large-leaved, green ivy

SMOKE TREE

Cotinus coggygria 'Flame'

A useful shrub with greyish-purple flowers and marvellous autumn leaves making it ideal for introducing another colour and a graceful leaf shape into both a mixed border and a flower arrangement.

type	Hardy deciduous shrub
flowers	Feathery, greyish-purple flowers in midsummer, hence its nickname
foliage	Ovate leaves, light green in spring, flame-coloured in autumn
height	4m (12ft)
planting	Autumn-spring
position	Full sun
soil	Ordinary, well-drained
care	To get the best autumn tints do not overfeed

propagation	Heel cuttings in autumn or by layering
varieties for flower arranging	*C. c.* 'Atropurpureus' has pinky-purple flowers and purple-tinged foliage

BOX

Buxus sempervirens 'Suffruticosa'

Box is one of the most useful shrubs for any time of year. In midsummer it can be preserved in glycerine and will go a light creamy colour; in winter, it can be added to festive greenery or used as a filler for garlands and swags.

type	Evergreen, small shrub
flowers	Insignificant
foliage	Small oval bright green leaves
height	1m (3ft)
planting	Autumn or spring
position	Sun or light shade
soil	Ordinary
care	Cut back to encourage bushy growth
propagation	Semi-hardwood cuttings
varieties for flower arranging	*B. s.* 'Handworthensis' is a vigorous evergreen shrub, good for hedging and ideal for plundering for flower arranging

OCTOBER

*Morning coffee in a sheltered spot in the garden in the autumn
sunshine and the delights of the bulb catalogue – these are the
pleasures of the month. It is a surprisingly buoyant time. Even
though it means the end of the annuals, and most herbaceous plants
are by now shrivelled and sad, there are so many positive tasks this
month to bring out the creative side of every gardener. There are
bulbs to choose and to plant. The selection for flower arranging is
vast, and some of the spring flowers like erythronium and leucojum
are not readily available from a florist. As well as making a
contribution to the garden they last well indoors. Others like
camassia and viridiflora tulips are valuable because they flower
later than most other spring bulbs.*

*Herbaceous plants can be divided to increase the stock or to swop
with friends, and this in itself is an encouraging task. Although we
can see evidence of the year's decline all around us, we can feel
cheerfully positive about the crop of blooms next year. This is also the
month to plant conifers and evergreens, while the ground is easy to
work and still warm. It will give the shrubs and trees a chance to
establish themselves before the onset of severe weather.*

*The dried material, carefully collected over the summer, can be
arranged along with preserved foliage for winter arrangements in the
home. In a late autumn, foliage will still absorb glycerine if the
leaves are in good condition and the sap is still rising early in the
month. It is worth trying a spray or two, if you did not get round to
doing it last month (see page 137). Beech foliage with its coppery
autumn tints turns a pleasant light bronze shade, quite a different
colour from the beech preserved in glycerine in early summer.
If country walks have to take the place of gardening, go searching for
driftwood.*

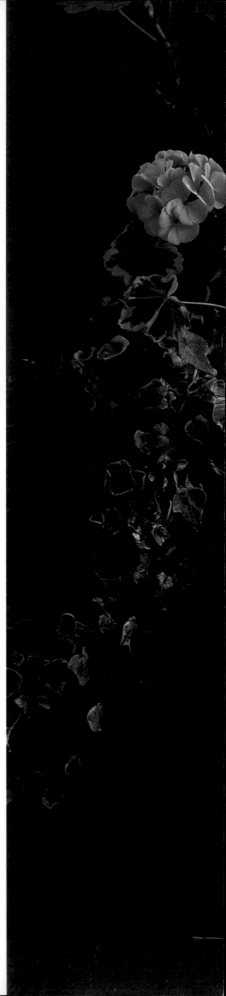

tasks

FOR THE

month

CHECKLIST

☐ Harvest seed heads for flower arranging
☐ Dig up dahlias when frost blackens their foliage
☐ Divide herbaceous perennials and rhizomes
☐ Plan, buy and plant bulbs for spring

MAINTENANCE

CUTTING DOWN

Once you have harvested all the seed heads that might be included in dried flower arrangements – poppies, thistles and any grasses, it is time to think about cutting down perennials to tidy the garden before the winter. If the foliage is still going to be of some use, however, you can leave cutting down any plants until the early spring. Personally I prefer to leave *all* grey-leaved plants. They can still look good during the winter and certainly better than a balding clump of twigs in a desert of bare earth. Others, like delphiniums, are by now straggly and the foliage is too soft to use. Once you have picked all the usable foliage on any plant, cut it down almost to the ground. At this stage, large, established clumps of plants can be divided to make more plants or to improve the quality of the flowers for next year.

DAHLIAS

Dahlias flower until the first frosts, this month or next, turn their foliage black. When this happens, cut the stems down, removing all the leaves to within 15cm (6in) of the tubers.

▪ Dig up the tubers carefully,

using a fork, trying to keep them intact. If any tubers get damaged accidentally, cut them off using a sharp knife.

PROPAGATION

DIVIDING HERBACEOUS PERENNIALS

▪ First dig the holes where you are going to transplant the divided pieces.
▪ Water the planting holes.
▪ Ease out the plant to be divided, keeping as big a root ball and as much soil intact as you can.
▪ Insert two forks, back to back and touching, right through the root ball. Ease the forks apart to divide the clump. This is often easier said than done. Very tough and matted root balls can be severed with a knife.
▪ The centre part of the clump is usually woody and should be discarded. Keep only the strong healthy growth.
▪ Re-plant in small sections, adding a handful of bonemeal at the roots.

Plants that can be divided

These fall into several different categories; the general principles are the same, but the method of severing the plant varies.

▪ Those with fibrous, spreading roots and several stems rising out of the crown that can be teased apart with the hands such as polyanthus.

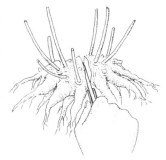

▪ Larger clumps and those with woody crowns and growth buds that will need two forks or even a knife to split them such as delphiniums and rudbeckia.

▪ Those that grow from tubers, such as peonies and dahlias (division of dahlias see page 38).
▪ Those that grow from rhizomes with a bud attached that will grow into new roots, such as border iris and montbretia.

DIVIDING A RHIZOME

▪ Select healthy, plump rhizomes with a fan of leaves attached.
▪ Cut off sections 5–7.5cm (2–3in) long. Discard the old centres.

▪ Re-plant horizontally, in a sunny site, and only barely below the surface of the soil. Irises should be divided after flowering in July.
▪ Remove the soil, label them and stand them upside down in a frost-free shed or cool greenhouse for several days to dry out the sap in the stems.
▪ After this, store them in shallow boxes on a bed of

HERBACEOUS PLANTS THAT DO NOT LIKE BEING DIVIDED OR DISTURBED:

Alstroemeria
Helleborus
Peonia
Romneya

(division of dahlias see page 38)

slightly damp peat, in an airy, cool shed or indoors in a cold room. Don't cover the crowns – the point where the tubers join the stem – as this is where the new growth appears. It avoids any tendency to soften or rot. The crowns can be dusted with flowers of sulphur as a precaution.

■ In a frost-free area in the garden, such as beneath a south- or west-facing wall, dahlias will survive the winter without being lifted, but should still be divided every few years.

PLANTING

BULBS FOR SPRING

A bulb is a minor miracle. Every year I think this when I see the dry, onion-like appearance of the bulbs in their boxes in the hardware shops compared with the glossy photograph above of their transformation in the spring.

A bulb is a storage organ, and everything the bulb needs in the way of food reserves is inside the overlapping fleshy scales. Sometimes these are protected inside a papery skin called a 'tunic', for example daffodils, or they have no outer covering, for example lilies (A and B). The base of the bulb is hardened stem tissue, known

as the basal plate. The roots emerge from its outer edges. A bulb is a permanent thing, that is, given the correct care, it produces flowers and leaves each successive year. They die down and the bulb then lies dormant for a period.

A corm is different. It is made of a solid mass (as opposed to scales) and is replaced each year by a new corm growing on top of the old one. It has a dry covering and a basal plate from which the roots grow (C).

Tubers, such as dahlias, are different again. Also a solid mass, they are swollen undergound *stems* and store the nutrients from one season's growth to start the plant growing again the following year. They have no basal plate and no tunic (D).

Rhizomes are thickened underground stems, with roots and leaf buds. The stems grow horizontally and sometimes very near the surface of the soil such as in the border iris (fig E).

Buying bulbs

If you are buying bulbs in a garden centre, choose the largest, firmest bulbs. They should have no bruise marks or mildew. Gently press them and discard those that feel even slightly flabby. The outer coats should be intact and the bulb should not be damaged or scored in any way.

If you buy by mail order, choose a reputable *specialist bulb nursery*. Bulbs are graded according to size and a rigorous check is kept on the quality of the bulbs. You will also discover bulbs you haven't grown before and, as bulbs provide the first and the last flowers of the year, you may even be able to lengthen the flowering period in your garden.

Growing bulbs

The first year it flowers, your bulb will do well as all the food reserves are in the swollen bulb that has been grown by an expert. In subsequent years it is up to you.

■ Bulbs **must** have well-drained soil. Like most other plants, they will not survive cold, waterlogged conditions.

■ Add a handful of peat mixed with bonemeal to the base of each planting hole.

■ Feed the bulbs with liquid feed, high in potash, when they begin to grow vigorously and at regular intervals until flowering has finished.

■ Never allow them to dry out completely, and give them plenty of water during the growing season.

■ Allow the foliage to die down slowly and naturally. Bending the leaves over and knotting them to make them look tidy may cut off the supply of nourishment to the bulb, just when it is needed to build it up for flowering next year. If the foliage is in the way keep it tidy with loose elastic bands around each bundle of leaves *without* bending over the tops. This keeps them from sprawling all over the soil. When the foliage has withered and turned yellow, the leaves are easily detached as one.

■ Store bulbs in a warm, dry place once they are lifted after the foliage has died.

BULBS TO PLANT IN THE AUTUMN

Allium – 5–7cm (2–3in) deep in well-drained soil and sun, flowers early to late summer

Alstroemeria Ligtu hybrids – 10–15cm (4–6in) deep in rich, sandy soil and full sun, flowers midsummer to early autumn

Arum italicum 'Pictum' 10–15cm (4–6in) deep in moisture-retentive soil and partial shade, grown for its leaves

Crown imperials (*Fritillaria imperialis*) – 10–15cm (4–6in) deep in fertile, well-drained soil, flowers mid- to late spring

Gladiolus nanus – 8cm (3in) deep in fertile soil, flowers early summer onwards

Guernsey lily (*Nerine bowdenii*) – (see p99), flowers early to mid-autumn

Harlequin flower (*Sparaxis*) – 10–12cm (4–5in) deep in a sheltered sunny site or under glass, flowers mid-spring to midsummer

Iris – bulbs 10cm (4in) deep, rhizomes just below soil surface, most prefer well-drained soil and sun, flowers spring to summer

Ixia – (see p58), flowers summer

Leucojum vernum 10cm (4in) deep in moisture-retentive soil, flowers mid-winter to early spring

Lily of the valley (*Convallaria majalis*) – 10cm (4in) deep in moist soil and partial shade, flowers mid- to late spring

Montbretia (*Crocosmia*) – 7cm (3in) deep in well-drained soil, now or in spring, flowers midsummer to early autumn

Narcissus – (see p23), flowers late winter onwards

Quamash (*Camassia*) – 20cm (8in) deep in good soil and light shade, flowers early summer

Snowdrop (*Galanthus*) – (see p14), flowers late winter and early spring

Tulips – (see p47), flowers mid-spring to midsummer

Winter aconite (*Eranthis hyemalis*) – (see p15), flowers early winter to early spring

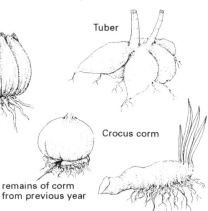

Scaly lily bulb

Tulip bulb with dry covering known as as a 'tunic'

remains of corm from previous year

Tuber

Crocus corm

Rhizome

plants
OF THE
month

CONEFLOWER
Rudbeckia fulgida 'Goldsturm'

Excellent flowers for cutting, in strongly vibrant colours, especially useful because they flower late in the summer. They are called coneflowers because of their dark domed centres.

type	Deciduous perennial
flowers	Daisy-type, with strap-shaped petals, black cone centres, long sturdy stems for flower arranging. Midsummer to early autumn
foliage	Narrow, lanceolate mid-green
height	60–90cm (2–3ft)
planting	In spring
position	Full sun
soil	Well-drained soil
care	Feed during flowering season. Support with twigs if necessary
propagation	By division or seed sown in autumn or spring
varieties for flower arranging	*R. laciniata* 'Golden Glow' is a double variety, up to 2.2m (7ft) tall, with pretty, deeply cut foliage

RED HOT POKER
Kniphofia 'Little Maid'

Although the well-known red hot poker is not as commonly grown in gardens these days, this smaller variety is useful in flower arrangements. It has an erect stem which, like that of the tulip, has a will of its own, curving gracefully when in water.

type	Evergreen perennial
flowers	Terminal spikes of tubular pale creamy-yellow in late summer
foliage	Sharp-edged, strap-shaped
height	60cm (24in)
planting	In autumn or spring
position	Full sun to light shade
soil	Well-drained soil
care	Remove faded flower spikes close to the base. Protect crowns with mulch over winter
propagation	By division in spring. Does not usually flower in the first year after dividing
varieties for flower arranging	*K.* 'Cool Lemon' has lemon-yellow flower spikes

HEUCHERELLA

Heucherella tiarelloides

With a smaller leaf and flower spike than the usual coarse-leaved heucherella, it is ideal for giving the final touches to an arrangement – adding looseness or delicacy.

type	Evergreen perennial
flowers	Tiny, bell-shaped, soft pink, in spikes on thin but strong stems, from late spring to midsummer
foliage	Very pretty, light green, useful all year
height	38cm (15in)
planting	In autumn or spring
position	Sun or light shade
soil	Any well-drained garden soil
care	Cut down flower spikes after flowering
propagation	By division in autumn or spring
varieties for flower arranging	*H. t.* 'Bridget Bloom' has delicate creamy-pink flowers

HELICHRYSUM

Helichrysum petiolare

A very useful decorative foliage, it is tender but easily propagated from one year to the next with cuttings. It will survive mild winters in a very sheltered corner and produce long sprays of felted grey leaves early in the year. Useful for trailing over the edge of tubs or hanging baskets, it can also be trained as a climber.

type	Evergreen sub-shrub
flowers	Insignificant
foliage	Round to ovate, downy silvery-grey
height	30cm (12in)
planting	Late spring
position	Sun to light shade
soil	Light, well-drained, fertile soil
care	Remove flowers to encourage leaf growth. Liquid feed fortnightly throughout summer, if grown in tubs
propagation	By semi-ripe cuttings late summer
varieties for flower arranging	*H.p.* 'Limelight' has yellow-green leaves; *H.p.* 'Variegata' has variegated yellow-grey leaves

practical
project
1

DRIED GARDEN
FLOWERS

YOU WILL NEED

An oblong block of dry oasis foam
(specially made for dried flowers,
available from a florist)

This winter display is a reminder of summer. Garden annuals are mixed with everlasting flowers and seedheads, against a background of beech, preserved with glycerine.

MATERIALS

The container
*A flat-bottomed copper planter,
10cm (4in) deep and 30cm (12in) wide*

Foliage
Preserved beech

Flowers
Bells of Ireland *(Molucella)*
Larkspur
Straw flower *(Helichrysum)*
Golden drumstick *(Craspedia globosa)*
Cloth of gold *(Achillea)*
Sweet William *(Dianthus barbatus)*
Paris daisy *(Chrysanthemum frutescens)*
Love-in-a-mist seed pods
Poppy *(Papaver)* seed pods
Giant thistle *(Centaurea macrocephala)*

▪ Wedge the dry foam lengthwise on its edge in the planter, so that it is a little higher than the rim. Use extra off-cuts of foam to make it firm, if necessary.

▪ Place a long spray of glycerined beech two thirds of the way towards the back of the foam and slightly off-centre to the left. Add two more of unequal length at each side and slightly towards the front, to form a triangular outline. Add a couple of shorter sprigs, back and front (fig 1a).

▪ Add three sprays of Bells of Ireland, following the same triangular outline. Do not use too much of this – it looks heavy because of the number of heads per stem and can overpower an arrangement.

▪ Add the larkspur next, keeping within the triangular outline of the beech. Cut some of the stems to vary the lengths and bring some pointing towards the front to avoid a flat, one-dimensional look.

▪ Add the wired bunches of straw flower, spaced throughout the outline, and short stems of golden drumstick and cloth of gold, cutting the stems to varying lengths.

▪ Add very short stems of Sweet William so that the heads conceal the oasis, and fill in any gaps front and back.

▪ Finally insert a few poppy seed heads, love-in-a-mist pods and seven thistle heads throughout the design, keeping the long stems to the top and sides and shortening a little those that are coming forwards (figs 1b).

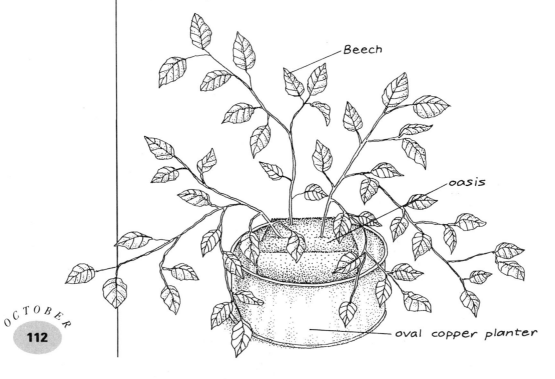

Beech

oasis

oval copper planter

Love in a mist seed pod

Straw flower

Golden drumstick

Poppy seed pod

Larkspur

Cloth of Gold

Giant Thistle

Bells of Ireland

Chrysanthemum

practical project *2*

'AUTUMN COLLECTION'

YOU WILL NEED

two blocks of oasis foam
oasis tape
two thick twisted branches of wood
large kidney shaped dark green base
pot containing ivy and a geranium

When the geraniums are brought in for the winter, don't cut them down too soon. Find a corner – a conservatory is ideal – to feature them in an autumn arrangement using the large patio pots. This arrangement uses one pot that stays as it is indoors for the winter months, containing ivy and a geranium, and an empty pot from which the annuals were removed. Very little foliage is used in this display, just a few sprigs of greenery to give a backing to the flowers and trails of the grey-leaved helichrysum to the front. The general idea is to give a 'tumble' of flowers flowing from the pot. The whole is nicely framed by the twisted branches of driftwood.

DRIFTWOOD

Any contorted or artistically shaped piece of wood has potential in a flower display. A huge piece can form a background for flowers, medium-sized pieces can be adapted to hold flowers and small pieces can be tucked in amongst them.

Treating driftwood

■ Rub away the soil, cut and scrape away any rotten parts and brush with a wire, or a very stiff, brush.

■ Scrub with disinfectant or mild household bleach. Weathered driftwood with a greyish bloom should not be scrubbed or the greyish tones will be lost.

■ Trim branches to a pleasing outline, removing crossing and spindly stems.

■ Leave the wood in its natural state. Alternatively, apply several coats of wax polish or linseed oil and rub hard to give a deep sheen. This darkens the wood slightly.

■ To give a greyish tinge, soak the wood for several days in a strong salt solution of 225g (1/2lb) salt dissolved in 4.5 litres (1 gallon) water. Leave in the sun to bleach.

■ Soak overnight in a strong solution of bleach – 1 litre (1 1/2 pints) bleach to 4.5 litres (1 gallon) water to get a yellowish tone in most woods. Light stain may improve the colour, but varnish gives a shiny, unpleasant and unnatural finish.

Supporting driftwood

Contorted pieces of wood usually have several different angles at which they can be placed. When you have decided on the best angle for a piece of wood, you will have to devise a way of making it stand.

■ Solid smaller pieces will need no support –

they can be placed lying flat amongst the flowers. Branches can be wedged into oasis or a pin holder, to stand them on end.

■ Driftwood clamps (ask at your flower club) or a small carpenter's clamp will support medium-sized pieces (fig 1).

■ Larger pieces will need to be permanently fixed to a base. This can be done by sawing the end of the wood across so that it is flat and securing it to a board, with a long screw from underneath (see page 24).

■ A 'leg' of dowelling can be glued to prop it at the correct angle (fig 2) or the wood can be permanently set in a mound of plastic filler that can be covered by foliage or moss (fig 3).

■ Very large pieces need to be set in a tub of cement. Wedge the end in a flower pot between two or three large stones. Pour in a thick mixture of ready-mix cement and allow it to set. Paint bucket and top of the cement a dark green so that it will blend into an arrangement (fig 4).

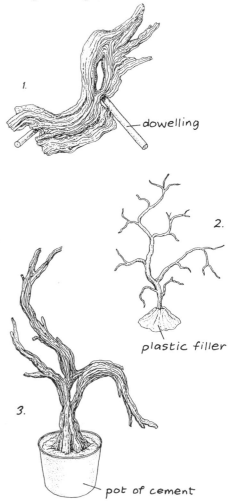

1.

dowelling

2.

plastic filler

3.

pot of cement

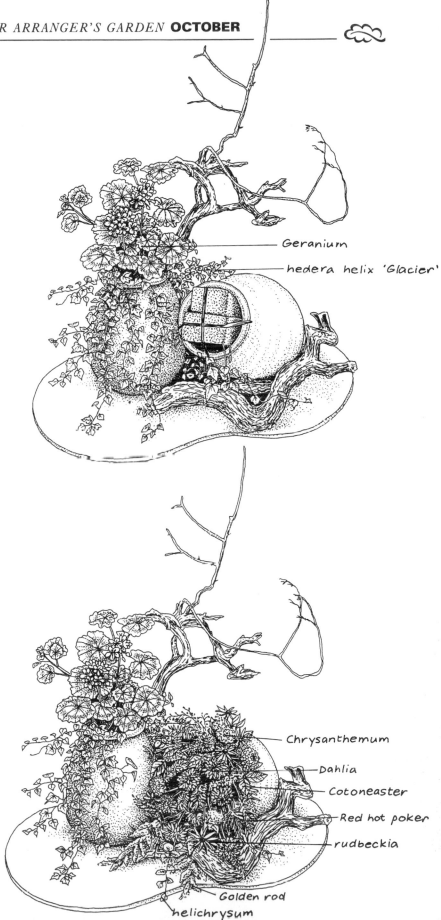

Geranium

hedera helix 'Glacier'

Chrysanthemum

Dahlia

Cotoneaster

Red hot poker

rudbeckia

Golden rod

helichrysum

● MATERIALS

The container
A terracotta, oil-jar shaped patio pot

Foliage
Cotoneaster × 'Cornubia'
Helichrysum petiolare

Flowers
Golden rod *(Solidago)*
Red hot poker *(Kniphofia* 'Little Maid')
Dahlia
Rudbeckia fulgida 'Goldsturm'
Chrysanthemum
Heucherella

■ Place the base in a corner. Place the branch supported in a pot with stones or cement (see p.114) towards the back, with the large pot of geraniums in front of it and to the left. Firmly wedge two large blocks of soaked oasis in the mouth of the empty pot and secure with tape. Lean this pot on its side, supported by a second branch, with the oasis to the front (fig 2a).
■ Insert short sprigs of cotoneaster to define the height of the arrangement to the back and to give an outline for the flowers.
■ Add a few trails of *Helichrysum petiolare* to the sides and front.
■ Insert stems of golden rod to flow from the base of the pot to the floor.
■ Following this outline, add spikes of red hot poker, bringing some forwards so that the arrangement is not flat and one-dimensional.
■ Insert dahlias, rudbeckia and chrysanthemums to fill in between the spikes of red hot poker, allowing the stems to droop downwards at the base.
■ Finally add spikes of heucherella throughout the design to lighten it (fig 2b).

NOTE

■ *Remove all the leaves from the stems of chrysanthemums when you arrange them. They die before the flowers and look bedraggled as well as introducing bacteria into the water* ■

NOVEMBER

This, to me, is the most dismal month of the year, both in the garden and for flower arranging. The hours of daylight dwindle, the roses cease to open, their buds stay frozen and waterlogged and, by the end of the month, the last of the glorious copper-coloured deciduous foliage has been swept away by the onslaught of the gales. There are compensations, though. This is a splendid time for hardwood cuttings. Both cadging and giving away cuttings of favourite shrubs is a sociable and friendly occupation this month.

Bulbs can still be planted. Each year, try to discover a new one, not just new varieties of the commoner bulbs, but some of the lesser-known bulbs, particularly the smaller ones. New hybrid lilies appear regularly, and looking through the bulb catalogue with its splendid photography can cheer up the bleakness of this time of the year quite a bit.

Container-grown plants can be planted when the weather is mild, as well as carnations and pinks, whose grey foliage is a pleasing addition at the front of a border. Sweet peas seedlings may need the protection of dried bracken – although with the shelter of a wall they seem to survive the searing wintery winds.

The dried flowers, preserved foliage and the seed heads you have carefully hoarded are another big compensation. It is very satisfying to make arrangements of your own garden flowers now when we need the colour and that cheerful reminder of the summer's produce. Arrangements from flowers and foliage you have preserved yourself are pleasing gifts and bring the growing season to a very satisfactory close.

tasks
FOR THE
month

CHECKLIST

- [ ] Take hardwood cuttings, for example, berberis, cotoneaster and roses
- [ ] Propagate clematis, magnolia and lilac by layering
- [ ] Prepare the soil and plant roses or heel them in if the ground is frosty
- [ ] Plant lilies
- [ ] Choose new shrubs for different leaf shapes

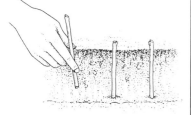

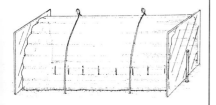

SHRUBS FOR HARDWOOD CUTTINGS

Berberis •
Cotoneaster • Deutzia •
Dogwood *(Cornus)* • Euonymus •
Forsythia • *Kerria japonica* •
Ligustrum • *Lonicera nitida* •
Mock orange *(Philadelphus)* •
Roses • Spirea • Tamarix •
Viburnum • Weigela

SHRUBS FOR LAYERING

Clematis • Forsythia • Lilac •
Magnolia • Rhododendron

PROPAGATION

HARDWOOD CUTTINGS

Take hardwood cuttings this month and next. If your soil is well-drained and sandy or gritty, taking hardwood cuttings is simply a matter of pushing prepared cuttings into the open ground. If you have clay soil, you will have a higher success rate by adding cuttings compost or sand to the soil. You do not need a propagator or greenhouse, but they take some time to root and so are not as exciting as semi-hardwood cuttings. You will not get a one hundred per cent success rate – just take plenty to compensate for this.

- First prepare a bed for the cuttings. Dig a V-shaped trench, about 10cm (4in) deep, in a sheltered part of the garden. Sprinkle coarse sand at the base of the trench.
- Choose shoots, 25–30cm (10–12in) long and about the thickness of a pencil, from the current year's growth of mature wood, which feels woody to the touch.
- Make a straight cut, just above a bud at the top and at an angle just below a bud at the bottom. Remove the leaves from the lower half of the cutting.

- Insert the cuttings against one side of the trench. Ideally, the top bud should be a little above ground level. Replace the soil and firm in gently.
- In a very severe winter, cover with a cloche. Leave the cuttings undisturbed for a year or longer until they have formed good roots and there is healthy top growth. Then they can be transplanted into a more permanent home.

LAYERING SHRUBS

This is another very simple way to propagate both evergreen and deciduous shrubs at this time of year. Some shrubs layer naturally as the low-trailing branches rub against the earth, causing a wound in the bark. A callus develops and from this roots begin to grow and anchor the branch. Where this does not occur naturally, it can be encouraged for shrubs with long, low-sweeping branches that touch the soil. The best time to layer shrubs is midsummer to early autumn.

- Choose a non-flowering, pliable branch that is long enough to touch the ground.
- Where the branch meets the ground make a a slanting cut half-way through the

stem. If evergreen, strip off the leaves for about 10cm (4in) each side of this cut.
- Scoop out the soil and bury the cut in 5cm (2in) of soil. Bend a florist's wire into a U-shape and push it into the ground over the cut to hold the branch in place.
- Cover this with compost or moist peat and do not allow the soil to dry out completely.
- Tie the branch to a short stake to prevent it from moving in the wind.

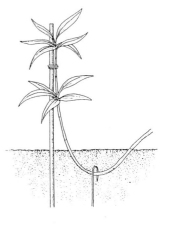

- Sever the newly rooted section from the parent plant with secateurs. Ornamental shrubs take between six months and a year to form good roots. Magnolias and rhododendrons may take up to two years.

PLANTING

ROSES

This is the best month to plant roses. The soil is still warm, encourages root growth and gives the rose a chance to establish before the spring. It will flower earlier than a spring-planted rose.

Preparing the soil

Roses like a neutral, fertile, well-drained soil, on the sandy side. If possible, site them in full sun. Treat the soil *in advance* of planting the rose bush — it pays dividends in healthy roses with more blooms. Soil treatments should be done very early in the month to allow the ground to settle before planting. Dig in any of these materials — well-rotted manure, leaf mould, garden compost, mushroom compost, ash from a bonfire or washed seaweed. They all will improve the soil structure and supply some nutrients.

Planting the roses

As a general guide plant hybrid tea roses 60cm (24in) apart and floribunda roses 75cm (30in) apart.

● Prepare the planting mixture. Fill a bucket with peat and mix two handfuls of bonemeal through it. Moisten the mixture. This is enough for four rose bushes.
● Cut off any damaged roots and prune the others to no more than 25cm (10in). Trim straggly side shoots and old flower heads. Immerse the roots in a bucket of water.
● Dig out a deep, wide hole, sufficiently wide to allow the roots to be spread out.
● Spread some of the planting mixture in the base of the hole, piling it up to a mound in the centre.
● Sit the rose on the mixture

and spread out the roots.
● Holding the rose steady with one hand, cover the roots with more planting mixture, fill up with soil.
● Tread the soil around the rose firmly with your feet.

MADONNA LILIES

The Madonna lily (*Lilium candidum*) should be planted early this month. It is one of the wonderful, old cottage garden lilies that underlines the truth that *most* lilies are extremely easy to grow. It used to be seen growing on allotments and even on neglected wasteland. A basal rooted lily (see page 82), it can sometimes be a little difficult to establish. Unlike other lilies, it likes lime and does not need shade, but like *all* lilies it prefers a rich, fertile soil and good drainage is important.

● Choose an open, sunny position, in slightly alkaline soil.
● Turn over the top layer of soil to a depth of 20cm (8in) and incorporate well-rotted manure and compost.
● Set the bulbs at a depth of only 5cm (2in).

PLANNING

PLANTING FOR LEAF SHAPES

Foliage is something you begin to love dearly as a flower arranger. Each new shrub is an exciting discovery and you begin to choose shrubs to grow, not for the flowering habits, but for the shape and texture of their leaves. The mature leaves of the glossy, dark green mahonia, with its prickly incisions at the leaf margins add a different dimension to a flower display than, say, the young blue-grey foliage of *eucalyptus gunnii* with its perfoliate leaf.

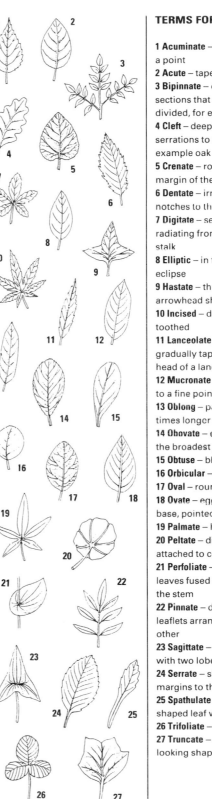

TERMS FOR LEAF SHAPES

1 Acuminate – tapers gradually to a point
2 Acute – tapers to a sharp point
3 Bipinnate – divided into several sections that are, in turn, sub-divided, for example mimosa
4 Cleft – deeply rounded serrations to the leaf edge, for example oak
5 Crenate – rounded teeth to the margin of the leaf
6 Dentate – irregularly toothed notches to the margin of the leaf
7 Digitate – several leaflets radiating from the top of the leaf stalk
8 Elliptic – in the shape of an eclipse
9 Hastate – three-pointed, arrowhead shape
10 Incised – deeply and sharply toothed
11 Lanceolate – narrow and gradually tapering, as with the head of a lance
12 Mucronate – oblong, tapering to a fine point at the tip
13 Oblong – parallel-sided, three times longer than wide
14 Obovate – egg-shaped, with the broadest part at the tip
15 Obtuse – blunt or rounded
16 Orbicular – disc-shaped
17 Oval – rounded oval
18 Ovate – egg-shaped at the base, pointed at the tip
19 Palmate – hand-shaped
20 Peltate – disc-shaped, stem attached to centre of the leaf
21 Perfoliate – two opposite leaves fused together around the stem
22 Pinnate – divided into pairs of leaflets arranged opposite each other
23 Sagittate – arrowhead shape, with two lobes pointing back
24 Serrate – sharply indented margins to the leaf
25 Spathulate – modified spoon-shaped leaf with tapered base
26 Trifoliate – three leaflets
27 Truncate – abrupt, stunted-looking shape

plants
OF THE
month

COTONEASTER
Cotoneaster franchetii

A useful rather than spectacular shrub for most of the year. Its curving branches are excellent for outlining the shape of an arrangement, and the bright winter berries are a bonus.

type	Evergreen or semi-evergreen shrub
flowers	Small, white pinky-tinged, unremarkable flowers in early summer. Orange-red berries in the autumn
foliage	Oval, grey-green, glossy leaves on graceful arching branches
height	2.5m (8ft)
planting	From mid-autumn to late winter
position	Sun or semi-shade
soil	Ordinary garden soil. Thrives in dry, sandy soil
care	Trim to keep in shape
propagation	By heel cuttings in late summer to early autumn
varieties for flower arranging	*C. f.* var. *sternianus* has sage-green leaves and orange-red berries

BERBERIS
Berberis aggregata 'Barbarossa'

A shrub that is at its best in autumn when weighed down with luscious berries. It has to be handled carefully because of the spines but it is valuable for flower arranging.

type	Semi-evergreen, arching shrub
flowers	Racemes of yellow flowers in late spring followed by waxy, pinky-red berries
foliage	Narrow, oval, dark green leaves
height	2m (6ft)
planting	Autumn to spring
position	Full sun to give best colour
soil	Ordinary
care	Remove old wood to ground level
propagation	Heel cuttings in late summer
varieties for flower arranging	*B.* x *stenophylla* is evergreen with golden-yellow flowers in spring and black fruit; *B. thunbergii* 'Atropurpurea' is deciduous with rich purple-red leaves

MEXICAN ORANGE BLOSSOM
Choisya ternata

A must for flower arranging because it has everything – delightful, glossy foliage that can look deceptively like flower heads in an arrangement. The leaves take up glycerine well and, although small, the white blossom is useful in arrangements.

type	Evergreen, hardy flowering shrub, needs shelter in colder areas
flowers	Small corymbs of white flowers that smell like orange blossom in late spring
foliage	Trifoliate, glossy, green, evergreen leaves
height	Up to 2m (6ft)
planting	In mid- to late spring
position	Full sun, shelter in cold areas
soil	Fertile, well-drained soil
care	Regular pruning is not necessary but prune to keep in shape and thin out immediately after flowering. If long branches are removed, new branches will grow from the base – ideal for the flower arranger
propagation	By semi-ripe cuttings in late summer
varieties for flower arranging	*C. t.* 'Sundance' has bright yellow leaves, each consisting of three leaflets

GRISELINIA
Griselinia littoralis

This shrub brings freshness and lightness into a shrub border with its glossy, apple-green leaves. It does the same in a flower display and is even more valuable in winter, contrasting with the darker green of most other evergreen subjects. The variegated form is just as useful.

type	Slightly tender, fast-growing, evergreen shrub
flowers	Tiny, inconspicuous flowers in spring
foliage	Delightful, apple-green, ovate-oblong leaves on stiff stems
height	Up to 6m (20ft)
planting	In autumn or spring
position	Sun or semi-shade
soil	Fertile, well-drained soil
care	Provide shelter from frost in cold areas
propagation	By heel cuttings in late summer or early autumn
varieties for flower arranging	*G.l.* 'Variegata' has bright green leaves splashed with grey-green and cream. It is less hardy, bushier and not as tall as *G. littoralis*

practical

project

1

ALL-FOLIAGE DESIGN

YOU WILL NEED

shallow saucers to hold oasis
a large block of oasis
foam, cut in half
oasis tape

When there are no flowers in the garden it is still possible to make a flower arrangement – only it will be called an all-foliage design! This arrangement of foliage from the late autumn garden shows just how much greenery is still available. Most of the leaves will remain in reasonable condition for use in the winter.

MATERIALS

The container
A large piece of driftwood, incorporated into the design

Foliage
New Zealand flax *(Phormium tenax* 'Variegatum')
Elaeagnus maculata
Griselinia littoralis
Mexican orange blossom *(Choisya ternata* 'Sundance')
Fern
Fig *(Ficus)*
(Golden privet *Ligustrum ovalifolium* 'Aureo-marginatum')
Hedera canariensis

Berries
Cotoneaster franchetii

■ Tape the soaked blocks of foam to the saucers. Place one to the front of the driftwood at the base and tape the other to sit securely on the driftwood, slightly raised and towards the back (fig 1a).

■ Insert three long spears of New Zealand flax in the oasis at the back of the display, following the soaring line of the driftwood.

■ Add a long curving branch of cotoneaster beside the New Zealand flax and a shorter one curving to the left. Insert a branch of cotoneaster in the other block of foam to curve towards the front.

■ Add a long stem of ivy to soften the upward line of the driftwood and others to the sides and front.

■ Fill in with sprigs of elaeagnus, griselinia and variegated privet.

■ Add large single leaves of fern low in the display and pointing left and towards the front (fig 1b).

■ Add a rosette of Mexican orange blossom to the centre to make the focal point of the arrangement with a smaller sprig higher in the design and a third trailing towards the front and to the right. Finally add single fig leaves at the back and front (fig 1c).

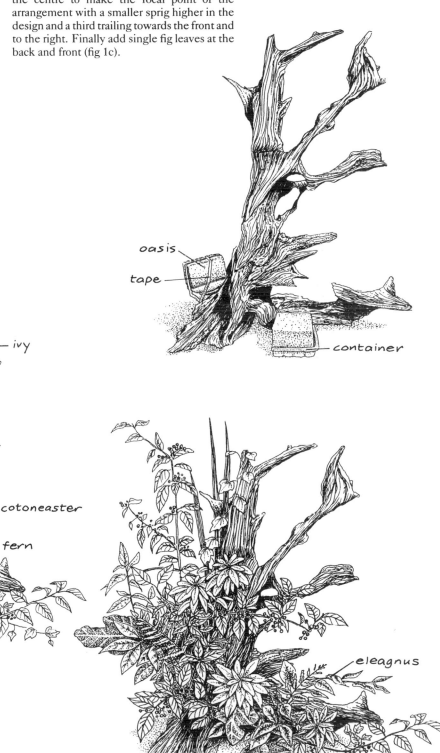

practical
project
2

MAKING A SWAG

YOU WILL NEED

dry oasis foam (sold as 'oasis sec')
2.5m (2¾yd) thick cord
florist's stem wire
brown velvet ribbon 5cm (2in) wide

NOTE

▪ You can also use a strip of pegboard or even thick card as a rigid backing of any length you choose, through which it is possible to insert wire or tape to hold dry oasis for the foliage. Remember that the finished length will be longer than the cork or board as the foliage will project beyond it ▪

Swags and wall plaques of dried or fresh material were more popular in Victorian times than they are today, but wall hangings are still an ideal way of brightening up a dull corner. Suspending flowers allows you to add decoration to the odd corner where there is no space for a pot of flowers.

This wall hanging is simply a collection of glycerined foliage which illustrates the subtle tones of sepia and brown that leaves take on once they have absorbed glycerine.

To make a more colourful swag, add in ever-lasting flower heads and short sprigs of dried garden annuals similar to those used in the dried flower arrangement of the previous month.

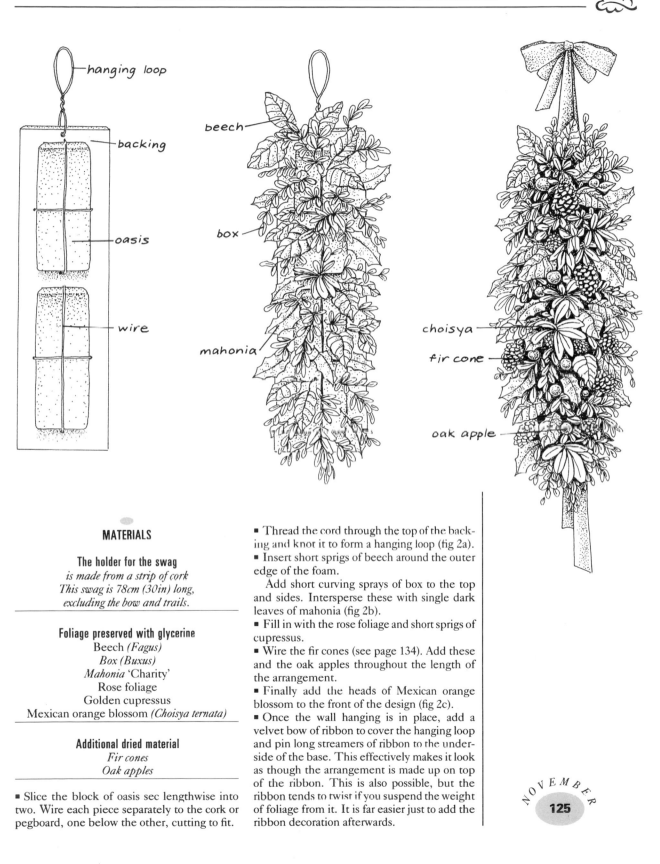

MATERIALS

The holder for the swag
is made from a strip of cork
This swag is 78cm (30in) long,
excluding the bow and trails.

Foliage preserved with glycerine
Beech *(Fagus)*
Box *(Buxus)*
Mahonia 'Charity'
Rose foliage
Golden cupressus
Mexican orange blossom *(Choisya ternata)*

Additional dried material
Fir cones
Oak apples

■ Slice the block of oasis sec lengthwise into two. Wire each piece separately to the cork or pegboard, one below the other, cutting to fit.

■ Thread the cord through the top of the backing and knot it to form a hanging loop (fig 2a).
■ Insert short sprigs of beech around the outer edge of the foam.
   Add short curving sprays of box to the top and sides. Intersperse these with single dark leaves of mahonia (fig 2b).
■ Fill in with the rose foliage and short sprigs of cupressus.
■ Wire the fir cones (see page 134). Add these and the oak apples throughout the length of the arrangement.
■ Finally add the heads of Mexican orange blossom to the front of the design (fig 2c).
■ Once the wall hanging is in place, add a velvet bow of ribbon to cover the hanging loop and pin long streamers of ribbon to the underside of the base. This effectively makes it look as though the arrangement is made up on top of the ribbon. This is also possible, but the ribbon tends to twist if you suspend the weight of foliage from it. It is far easier just to add the ribbon decoration afterwards.

DECEMBER

This is a delightful month for flower arrangers, not so much for arranging flowers as for arranging foliage. Those wonderful evergreens – holly, spruce, juniper, ivy, cedar, laurel – all the traditional, seasonal greenery. The leaf shape and splendour of some of the evergreens shows up starkly against the bare twigs of neighbouring deciduous shrubs. Take a closer look at the variegated elaeagnus whose green and yellow markings look like brush strokes made by an amateur. The apple green of griselinia and the common golden privet is much appreciated this month.

On the gardening front, the weather is usually open enough to give several days in the week when it is still possible to work in the garden, even though activities are curtailed by the shortening days and early morning frosts. But it is a good month for getting the circulation going, with a spot of digging on lighter soils and tidying flower beds or preparing new ones. It is the month for the winter bulbs, the paper-white narcissi – the most rewarding bulb to grow for those with little patience, as it can be in flower within six weeks of planting – and the essential, fragrant hyacinth. Once the hyacinths are in flower, try incorporating the bowls of bulbs into a group of low-growing or trailing houseplants. The additional foliage helps their rigid stems and often shows them off to better advantage than a solitary bowl on a table, which can sometimes look quite stark.

Flowers are in short supply, although the early hellebores and winter-flowering jasmine are invaluable this month. If the weather has been mild and you have not cut your rose bushes back to half, in some areas there are a few brave rose buds clinging to the stem. Unless you have a heated greenhouse you may need to visit your florist for the traditional red carnations to supplement a seasonal display.

tasks
FOR THE
month

CHECKLIST

- [ ] Plan new shrubs and evergreens for your garden
- [ ] Heel in any newly bought shrubs and roses
- [ ] Prepare the ground for future planting
- [ ] Plant bare-rooted shrubs
- [ ] Protect shrubs and evergreens from icy weather

PLANNING

If the weather is at all reasonable, it is still possible to plant hardy shrubs, evergreens and bare-rooted stock. In fact, the beginning of this month is often the best time for evergreens as open weather in early winter is a better time to plant than bad weather in late autumn or early spring. You may have no choice, anyway, if you are given plants as presents.

EVERGREENS

Evergreens are invaluable to give shape and definition to the garden in winter when deciduous trees and shrubs are only stark outlines or traceries of branches. They are even more indispensable for a flower arranger's garden and some, like *elaeagnus maculata*, are stand-bys all year round. A basic planting of evergreen shrubs with attractive and useful foliage is needed so that there is always something in the garden from which to make a winter display. It also means that the flower arranger will never be short of foliage for any other month of the year.

Container-grown shrubs from a nursery
This is the most popular way of buying shrubs because you can see quite clearly

what you are buying. Be selective, look for good strong stems and healthy foliage. Don't buy the biggest, buy the healthiest, with a good branching habit, not thin long wands of stems. Do not buy any shrub with diseased or eaten leaves.

Balled shrubs
These are shrubs dug up at the nursery with the soil still around the roots so that they have minimum root disturbance. They are packaged for ease of carrying in sacking or nylon mesh. Again, you can see what you are buying and you can also judge from the roots how healthy the shrub is. Lift the plant supporting the weight of the ball so as not to disturb the roots and displace the soil.

Bare-rooted shrubs
Bare-rooted stock is readily available over the winter. These are plants dug up and sold in their dormant state without any soil at the roots and are cheaper than a similar container-grown variety. Packed in straw or damp peat, either singly or in bundles for mass planting, they are a good, inexpensive way of buying a quantity of plants for a hedge. Do not buy bare-rooted plants that have dried out at the roots or if the leaf buds are beginning to open out.

Pre-packaged shrubs
These are sold by

supermarket chains, sometimes even in garage forecourts. Unless you buy them very soon after delivery to the shop and you can see quite clearly that they have not been forced into premature growth by the humidity inside the plastic wrapper, they are not, usually, the best buy.

PLANTING

Planting is the most important operation in the garden at any time of year. But with winter planting it is even more essential to give the plants the best start and aftercare so that they have the best chance of survival.

Heeling in
The advantage of buying container-grown and balled plants is that they can be left until the weather conditions are right, as long as the soil is not allowed to dry out. Bare-rooted plants can be heeled in temporarily, in a sheltered spot in the garden, until the weather improves.
- Dig a shallow trench, lay the plants in it at an angle so that the wind does not blow them over.
- Cover the roots with topsoil.

Mail-order roses
Roses can still be planted if the ground is free from frost and not waterlogged. If planting has to be delayed for any reason, open the roses from their packing and heel them in, in any sheltered corner of the garden – even a herb bed near the house or a large flower tub, where the annuals have been cleared, will offer a temporary home until conditions are more suitable. Container-grown roses should be left in their containers in a sheltered frost-free spot until the weather is suitable for planting.

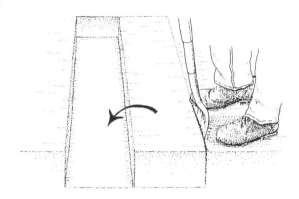

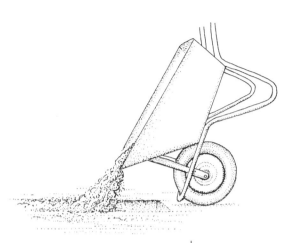

DIGGING

Digging is necessary on most soils to prepare it for planting. The best time to dig over the soil is in late autumn and early winter, before the onset of the worst of the weather. Digging is useful because
■ it improves drainage
■ it exposes soil to frost and fluctuating wet and dry conditions which break down the lumps over the winter
■ it introduces air into the soil and encourages the bacteria to become active so that the natural process of humus decay is speeded up
■ it is a chance to incorporate organic matter and fertilisers into the soil.

Single digging

There is a thorough and logical way of digging.
■ First spread the rotted manure, garden compost or other organic matter over the surface of the flower bed to be dug, at about one barrowload for every 8 square metres (9½ square yards).
■ Next use a sharp spade and insert it vertically to dig out a trench about 25cm (10in) to the full depth of the spade. Pile this soil in a wheelbarrow and transport

it to the back of the area to be dug.
■ Dig out a second trench and pile this soil into the space made by the first.
■ Dig over the ground in successive trenches and when you come to the end of the bed, fill the last trench with the soil from the first, which is in the wheelbarrow.

Double digging

This is more necessary in the vegetable garden than in the flower arranger's garden, except perhaps for growing sweet peas. It involves an extra process, forking over the compacted layer at the base of each trench.

Planting container-grown and balled plants
■ Prepare a planting mixture of one bucket of topsoil, one of moist peat, and two handfuls of bonemeal.
■ Dig a hole sufficiently large to take the plant and roots easily, with about 5cm (2in) of space at the sides.
■ Sprinkle a 7cm (3in) layer of planting mixture in the base of the hole. Lower the plant into the hole and remove the plant from its wrappings with as little disturbance as possible. If the roots are compacted, gently separate them at the ends.

■ Fill the space with the planting mixture, firming it as you fill. Finally, gently tread the soil around the plant with your feet.
■ Water the plant.

Planting bare-rooted shrubs
■ Plant as for roses, watering the planting hole and soaking the roots first (see page 119). Spread the roots out well, around the base of the planting hole.

MAINTENANCE

EVERGREENS

Keep newly planted subjects well watered. Evergreens may need further protection, depending on the site, until they are well established. Cover the roots with straw or peat and erect a screen of mesh, not a solid screen, to give some shield from icy winds. Use a general fertiliser in spring.

Firming

Strong winds can disturb plants, especially newly planted subjects, causing a gap in the soil around the stem where water may collect and freeze and may kill the plant. Firm the soil around vulnerable plants after a gale and when it is dry.

LIFE IN THE SOIL

Top soil *is the living, fertile, active top portion of the soil. It contains humus, supporting countless bacteria that change the materials in the soil into food for the plants. This is the layer that is turned over. With single digging, the dead, lifeless layer of soil underneath, known as the* **sub soil** *(recognisable as it is lighter in colour), should not be brought to the surface.*

EVERGREEN SHRUBS FOR THE FLOWER ARRANGER

Box (Buxus)
Camellia
Ceanothus
Choisya
Conifers, green and yellow varieties
Elaeagnus
Escallonia
Eucalyptus
Euonymus
Fatsia
Hebe
Laurel also *japonica*, the spotted variety (Aucuba)
Lonicera nitida
Mahonia
Privet, green and gold varieties (Ligustrum ovalifolium)
Pyracantha
Rhododendron
Rosemary
Rue (Ruta)
Skimmia
Viburnum

plants
OF THE
month

WINTER-FLOWERING JASMINE
Jasminum nudiflorum

Winter-flowering jasmine is a delightful shrub. It grows anywhere, flowers prolifically and the arching sprays of glossy, trifoliate leaves are as useful to the flower arranger in the summer as the flowers are in the winter. Cut some bare twigs of jasmine in late autumn, once the buds are showing, keep them in water in a warm room and watch them burst into a cascade of tiny golden flowers along the stem.

type	Hardy, deciduous, climbing shrub
flowers	Star-like, bright yellow, on slender, green leafless shoots from late autumn to early spring
height	Up to 3m (10ft)
planting	In mid-autumn to mid-spring
position	Any aspect. Needs support. Best against a fence or wall, but can be allowed to trail down a bank
soil	Any garden soil
care	Prune immediately after flowering as it flowers on new wood. Tie in new shoots
propagation	By hardwood cuttings in autumn

CHRISTMAS ROSE
Helleborus niger

The delicacy of the hellebore's white petals and yellow anthers are a joy to discover in the short, grey days of early winter. My hellebore always has plenty of buds opening for the festive season, and it can have no better companion than wands of the yellow-flowering jasmine and a background of holly. The stems of hellebores do not like floral foam – they wilt and need special treatment when arranging them (see page 132).

type	Evergreen perennial
flowers	White, open-faced, with yellow anthers from early winter to early spring
height	*H. niger* 30cm (12in); *H. orientalis* 45cm (18in)
planting	In mid-autumn
position	Partial shade, although *H. niger* also thrives, and flowers early, if planted in a sunny spot
soil	Fertile, well-drained soil
care	Once planted, hellebores do not like to be disturbed. Protect the white buds of *H. niger* with a cloche to prevent marking in bad weather. This also helps to lengthen the stems
propagation	By division in early spring
varieties for flower arranging	*H. orientalis* (Lenten rose) has pink, white or pale purple saucer-shaped flowers in late winter; *H. foetidus* (striking hellebore) has crowded panicles of yellow-green flowers in late winter to early spring

varieties for flower arranging	*I. aquifolium* 'Golden King' is, despite its name, a female shrub; *I. aquifolium* 'Silver Queen' is a male shrub – a conical tree with a silver margin to the leaves and red berries

LONICERA
Lonicera nitida 'Baggesen's Gold'

Planted in full sun, this is the golden shrub of winter. Plant it where it can be seen from the house in wintry sunshine. Useful to the flower arranger at any time of year, in winter it is a perfect partner to all the early bulbs and later to daffodils.

type	Bushy evergreen shrub
flowers	Insignificant
foliage	Tiny, golden-yellow oval leaves
height	1.5m (5ft)
planting	In mid-autumn to early spring
position	Full sun to give fresh golden leaves
soil	Any ordinary, well-drained soil
care	If used for hedging it can be cut regularly for flower arranging until mid-autumn. Mulch with leaf mould in spring
propagation	By hardwood cuttings in mid autumn. Can be layered in the autumn
varieties for flower arranging	*L. n.* 'Yunnan' has larger leaves and is a more upright shrub

HOLLY
Ilex

There are over 300 species of holly, from the common hedging holly *(Ilex aquifolium)* with glossy dark green leaves and sharp spines, to the yellow-berried holly (hedgehog holly), weeping holly and hollies with smooth leaves and no berries. The most useful for the flower arranger are those with white, cream or yellow variegation to the leaves; the berries are of secondary importance.

type	Evergreen shrub
flowers	Insignificant
height	'Golden King' 6m (20ft); 'Silver Queen' 5m (16ft)
planting	In spring or autumn, or any time in winter when conditions are suitable. Plant male and female shrubs together to aid pollination for berry production
position	Sun or shade. Sunny position gives better variegation
soil	Ordinary, well-drained, garden soil
care	If variegated hollies revert to green, remove all green shoots immediately from the base
propagation	By semi-ripe cuttings in late summer to early winter. Can also be layered

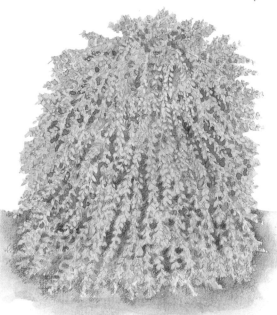

practical project *1*

'FESTIVE LUNCH'

YOU WILL NEED

five tall, slender red or green flower candles

FOAM HATERS
Hellebores do not like floral foam. The soft stems do not absorb water and wilt. The small, black, plastic, cylindrical containers from a roll of film (or a clear plastic lid from an aerosol can) are an ideal size to hold them. Push two or three containers about half way into the foam so that they are hidden by the greenery. Keep them well topped up with water.

This is a classic table arrangement for a festive occasion and is guaranteed to give a lot of pleasure. It lasts for a long time, just renewing the jasmine and hellebores as they need it. It is also very quick and easy to do.

MATERIALS

The container
A round flat dish, 15cm (6in) diameter, with soaked oasis cut to fit

Foliage
short tips from branches of spruce or fir
variegated holly
Griselinia littoralis

Flowers
Christmas rose (Helleborus niger)
Winter-flowering jasmine (Jasminum nudiflorum)
Ivy (Hedera helix 'Glacier')

■ Push the candles securely into the centre of the foam. Arrange flat sprays of fir around the sides of the base (fig 1a).

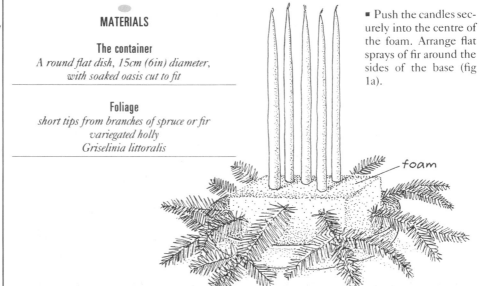

■ Insert short sprigs of variegated holly to cover the foam, and a few sprigs of griselinia to make a contrast in leaf shape and colour.
■ Push the small containers of hellebores into the foam, close to the base of the candles (see 'Foam Haters').
■ Finally, add spikes of winter-flowering jasmine, slightly longer than the outline of greenery, and a few lengths of ivy to trail over the table (fig 1b).

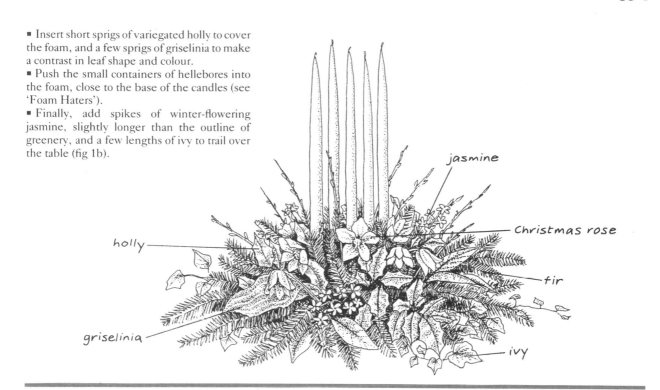

jasmine

Christmas rose

holly

fir

griselinia

ivy

practical
project
2

'WELCOME'

YOU WILL NEED

36cm (14in) diameter oasis ring
a bundle of stub wires from a florist

A welcome ring of mixed evergreens hanging on the door is an old tradition. It is a symbol of renewal and friendship. The custom is said to originate from Scandinavia and has both pagan and Christian associations.

You can buy the foundation wreath ring, ready filled with foam, from a florists. The secret is to get contrast and interest into the greenery by using a variety of textures and forms. In a small arrangement like this wreath you will not need as many contrasts as in a garland, for example, but a wreath of holly alone looks very uninteresting. If holly berries are scarce use rose hips, hawthorn or pyrancantha as well as artificial berries. Any silk flowers, ribbons or decorations look better kept together to the base of the ring, or it can end up looking 'spotty' and untidy.

practical project *2*

'WELCOME'
continued

MATERIALS

The container
A foundation wreath

Foliage
*Variegated holly, Ivy
Laurel, Yew, Spruce*

Trims
*Pine cones
Artificial or real berries
Silk poinsettia
Wide, gold-edged Offray ribbon*

- Soak the ring until the oasis will absorb no more water. Bend a wire over the ring and twist the ends together to form a hanging loop.
- Cut the sprigs of greenery 5–10cm (2–4in) in length, with a slanting cut so that the ends will pierce the oasis without crumbling it. Insert sprays of spruce around the outer and inner edges of the ring, positioning some pointing forwards at an angle (fig 2a).

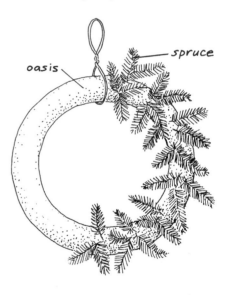

- Fill in the ring with the other sprigs of greenery, until the oasis is completely covered.
- Wire each fir cone by twisting a stub wire around the base and insert the wires into the oasis (fig 2b).

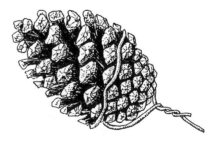

- Insert the groups of berries through the foliage. Place the poinsettia in a group at the base and add trims such as large bow, bells and wired trails of gold-edged ribbon to hang below the ring (fig 2c).

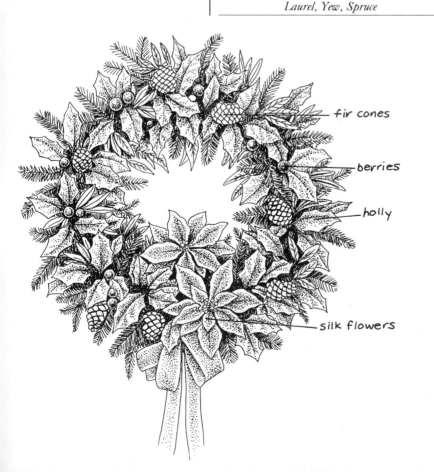

fir cones

berries

holly

silk flowers

Garlands can be made with either a plastic garland cage to hold the floral foam or a two-in-one garland frame – both obtainable from a florist. This is 2m (7ft) long and is made of double-sided sections – one side for fresh greenery and flowers and the other for making a garland of dried or silk material.

MATERIALS

The frame
a garland frame

For the centrepiece
A large block of soaked oasis in a flat oblong dish
5 candles in oasis candle holders
Artificial or fresh fruit and walnuts

Foliage
A selection from your garden of different leaf shapes and texture for example
Elaeagnus, Laurel, Spruce, Holly, Golden cupressus
Cedar (*Cedrus atlantica* 'Glauca' is particularly good)
Yew
Lonicera nitida
Variegated ivy
Euonymus

Trims
Red and green tartan ribbon
Fir cones

practical project *3*

A SEASONAL
GARLAND

■ Cut the garland holder in two. Work on both halves of the garland at the same time. Cut the foliage into short sprigs, 5–7.5cm (2–3in) long. Using flat leaves such as laurel as the background, insert the first foliage at intervals along the length of the garland (fig 3a).

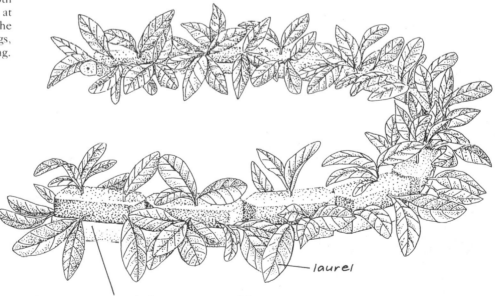

laurel

garland frame in sections

practical
project
3

A SEASONAL
GARLAND
continued

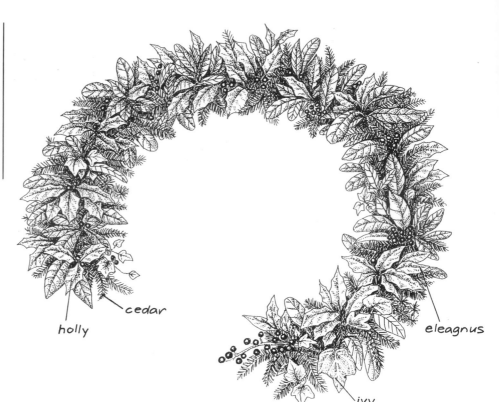

holly

cedar

eleagnus

ivy

■ Alternate with other leaves and sprigs of foliage and holly, evenly spaced until all the oasis is hidden (fig 3b). Add wired cones and wired loops of ribbon.

■ Place the oasis and holder in the centre of the mantelpiece. Insert five candles in secure oasis candle holders. Vary the height of the candles, as in the photograph, by cutting a little from the base of one or two.

Insert short branches of spruce, and sprigs of holly and ivy, keeping them low and well away from the candles.

■ Group a selection of fruit at the base of the candles, anchoring some of them on cocktail sticks or stub wires. Scatter nuts and small fir cones over the fruit.

■ Drape a garland at each side of the centre-piece to hang over the edge of the mantelpiece. Add loops and trails of tartan ribbon with variegated ivy at each end (fig 3c).

appendix

*CONDITIONING
FLOWERS AND
FOLIAGE*

A good flower arranger learns through practice. A satisfying arrangement needs quite a bit of planning time beforehand – to decide on a harmonious colour scheme and a pleasing combination of shapes in foliage and flowers. Once these have been chosen, the actual making up of the arrangement also takes time. Even when you are working on the display, more concentrated thought is needed to achieve satisfying proportions and a pleasing balance of all the component parts. Because of all this effort which goes into making a flower arrangement, not to mention the cost of the plants and containers, you will want the flowers and foliage to last for as long as possible. For this reason all plant material is treated before using it for flower arranging.

This process is known as *conditioning*, that is getting the flowers and leaves into as good a condition as possible so that they will last for the longest possible time. It is a continuing process starting with the picking and going on to caring for the flowers once they have been arranged.

CONDITIONING FLOWERS

- Pick flowers early in the morning, when the stems are turgid or in the cool of the evening, when they contain the most food reserves.
- Choose good specimens without blemishes.
- Plunge the stem ends immediately into 8–10cm (3–4in) of tepid water. This is absorbed by the plant more readily than cold water and contains less oxygen which might cause air blocks in the stem.
- Allow the flowers to stand in the water for at least two hours, preferably overnight, in a cool shady place.

CONDITIONING FOLIAGE

- Pick the foliage as above. Cut the stem ends on a slant to get the biggest surface area for water uptake.
- For mature, evergreen foliage and single leaves such as ivy and bergenia submerge the entire foliage in water for at least two hours. Foliage can take in water through the surface tissue. Do *not* submerge grey foliage as it loses its downy sheen.
- Slit the ends of hard stems with a knife.
- Scrape off the bark of woody stems at the stem end for about 2.5cm (1in).
- Treat young and soft foliage the same way as flowers.

SPECIAL TREATMENT

De-foliation
Lilac and mock orange *(Philadelphus)* last longer if all the leaves are removed before arranging. This allows the flowers to take up the maximum of water. Chrysanthemum leaves are also best removed, as they die before the flowers and this encourages bacteria.

Boiling
Branches of blossom, roses, mock orange *(Philadelphus)* and lilac last longer if the stem ends are boiled before arranging. Keep an old saucepan for this as some stems exude a poisonous substance. Put about 5cm (2in) of water into the pan and bring it to the boil. Hold the stem ends at the same level and plunge them into the water for about ten seconds. Shield the blossom from the steam with the pan lid or slip the heads inside a plastic bag. Then plunge the stem ends immediately into tepid water to condition for two hours.

Singeing
Some stems, such as euphorbias and poppies, exude a milky latex. Not only can this be an irritant, but it seals the stem end as it dries, preventing the uptake of water. Hold the stem end in a gas or candle flame until it chars. Leave them to condition in water as before. Poppies last well given this treatment.

Filling stems
Stems of lupins and delphiniums are hollow. It is possible to prolong their life by upturning the flower and filling the stem with water using a small funnel placed in the end. Plug the end with cotton wool or a small piece of crumbled oasis, which acts as a wick.

Spraying
The process of conditioning continues for the life of the flower. Top container up with water as necessary, and spray the entire arrangement with water daily.

Flower foods
The small packets of flower foods now sold by florists as crystals or liquids, contain substances to raise the acidity of the water. This decreases the chances of air blocks and is also said to help maintain the balance between evaporation and absorption. It discourages the growth of bacteria – the chief cause of premature wilting. Lemonade is a less efficient form of plant food. It has no anti-bacterial agents and in the proprietary food the sugars are balanced.

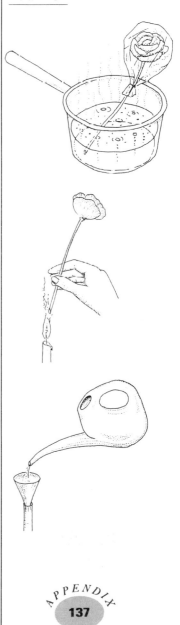

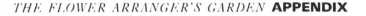

appendix

PRESERVING FOLIAGE WITH GLYCERINE

FOLIAGE TO GLYCERINE

Beech (Fagus) – Midsummer beech turns a very dark green, autumn beech goes a coppery-brown in 10 days–2 weeks
Box (Buxus) – Light gold in 3–4 weeks
Choisya – Dark gold in 4 weeks
Cupressus (golden varieties) – Light brown in 2–3 weeks
Camellia – Very dark brown in 3–4 weeks
Eucalyptus – Grey in 2–3 weeks
Fatsia – Dark brown, submerge single leaves in 4 weeks
Laurus nobilis – Dark brown in 3 weeks
Mahonia – Varies from light to mid-brown in 3–4 weeks
Oak (Quercus) – Mid-brown in 1–2 weeks
Pear (Pyrus) – Mid-brown in 1 week
Rose – Dark green in 1–2 weeks

Branches of beech leaves, arranged in a copper jug, are still the traditional foliage of winter. Preserved in glycerine, they last for years. The long sprays of beech are invaluable in winter arrangements mixed with fresh or realistic silk chrysanthemums, and the shorter branches are a perfect backing for dried and everlasting flowers.

Almost all foliage can be preserved in the same way, in glycerine and, although not all of it is beautiful when it is done, it is worth trying any type of foliage. The results vary a good deal according to the time of year and the maturity of the leaves when picked.

All glycerined foliage changes colour. Most of it turns varying shades of brown, some turns cream and rose foliage varies from green to greeny-brown. Standing cream foliage in strong sunshine will lighten it even further.

Beech is a good example – early in the year the bright green beech turns a very acceptable shade of dark green that goes well with dried flowers. Midsummer beech turns an even darker green, and beech beginning to turn brown in the autumn turns a delightful russet brown. The very early soft growth of the spring beech is too immature to glycerine and in very late autumn, once the sap has stopped rising, the beech will not absorb the glycerine.

Once foliage has absorbed glycerine it is virtually indestructible. It can be washed and if it is stored away for the summer and becomes crushed, it can even be ironed!

Foliage is of great value to the flower arranger to add to winter displays – it softens the inevitably stiff appearance of dried garden flowers. It no longer absorbs moisture and will come to no harm used in water with fresh flowers when foliage is scarce.

MATERIALS

a bottle of glycerine
a glass jug
hot water
jam jars
sprays of foliage, for example
beech, mahonia, fatsia

- Glycerine is used in the proportion of one part glycerine to two parts hot water. Pour a bottle of glycerine into an unbreakable glass jug. Fill the bottle twice with hot water and stir it briskly into the glycerine.
- Divide the diluted glycerine into jam jars and stand the sprays of foliage in 5cm (2in) of the solution. Trim sprays of beech to a good outline shape by removing excess leaves. Large

single leaves of mahonia and fatsia can be laid flat and immersed in glycerine.

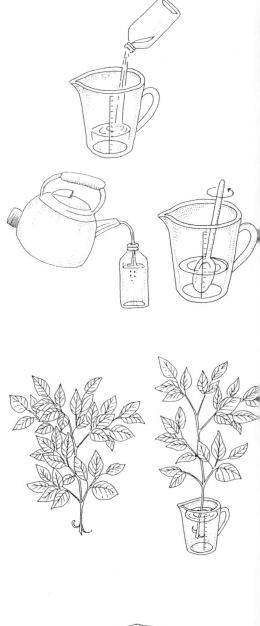

GARDEN FLOWERS FOR ARRANGING

Filled bars (■) are shaded; outline bars (□) are open.

Flowering season ▶	early spring	mid-spring	late spring	early summer	mid-summer	late summer	early autumn	mid-autumn	late autumn	early winter	mid-winter	late winter
LIME-GREEN												
Hacquetia	■											■
Euphorbia palustris & *epithymoides*	■	■	■									
Helleborus foetidus & *corsicus*	■	■	■									
Bells of Ireland *(Moluccella)*				■	■	■						
Lady's mantle *(Alchemilla mollis)*				■	■	■						
Love-lies-bleeding *(Amaranthus)*				■	■	■						
Nicotiana alata 'Lime Green'				■	■	■	■					
Zinnia var. 'Envy'				■	■	■						
WHITE												
Narcissus	□	□	□									
Stocks	□	□	□	□	□	□						
Tulips	□	□	□									
Pyrethrum			□	□								
Solomon's seal *(Polygonatum)*			□	□								
Candytuft *(Iberis)*				□	□							
Canterbury Bell *(Campanula)*				□	□	□						
Columbine *(Aquilegia)*				□	□							
Dahlia				□	□	□	□	□	□			
Gladiolus				□	□	□	□	□	□			
Bearded iris				□	□	□						
Madonna lily				□	□	□						
Peonia lactiflora				□								
Phlox				□	□							
Aster						□						
Anemone japonica							□	□	□			
Chrysanthemum maximum							□	□	□			
Helleborus niger & *orientalis*	□	□	□							□	□	□
MIXED COLOURS												
Stocks	■	■	■	■	■	■						
Roses			■	■	■	■	■	■	■			
Alstroemeria				■	■	■						
Columbine *(Aquilegia)*				■	■	■						
Gladiolus				■	■	■	■	■	■			
Snapdragon *(Antirrhinum)*				■	■	■						
Sweet peas *(Lathyrus)*				■	■	■						

GARDEN FLOWERS FOR ARRANGING

Flowering season ▶	early spring	mid-spring	late spring	early summer	mid-summer	late summer	early autumn	mid-autumn	late autumn	early winter	mid-winter	late winter
Annual chrysanthemum					■	■	■					
Perennial chrysanthemum						■	■					

BLUE AND PURPLE

	early spring	mid-spring	late spring	early summer	mid-summer	late summer	early autumn	mid-autumn	late autumn	early winter	mid-winter	late winter
Corm anemone	■	■	■									
Anemone pulsatilla	■	■										
Bulb iris	■	■	■									
Stocks	■	■	■	■	■	■						
Allium				■	■	■						
Asters				■	■	■						
Canterbury bells *(Campanula medium)*				■	■	■						
Clary *(Salvia sclarea)*				■	■	■						
Clematis				■	■	■						
Cornflower *(Centaurea)*				■	■	■						
Dahlia				■	■	■	■	■	■			
Delphinium and Larkspur				■	■	■						
Gladiolus				■	■	■	■	■	■			
Himalayan poppy *(Meconopsis)*				■	■	■						
Bearded iris				■	■	■						
Lupins				■	■	■						
Mullein *(Verbascum)*				■	■	■						
Scabious				■	■	■	■	■				
Sweet peas *(Lathyrus)*				■	■	■						
Veronica				■	■	■						
African lily *(Agapanthus)*					■	■	■					
Bear's breeches *(Acanthus mollis)*					■							
Gay feather *(Liatris)*							■					

PINKS AND REDS

	early spring	mid-spring	late spring	early summer	mid-summer	late summer	early autumn	mid-autumn	late autumn	early winter	mid-winter	late winter
Primulas	■	■	■	■	■	■						
Stocks	■	■	■	■	■	■						
Tulips	■	■	■									
Bleeding heart *(Dicentra)*		■										
Pyrethrum			■	■								
Allium				■	■	■						
Asters				■	■	■	■					
Astilbe				■	■	■						
Candytuft *(Iberis)*				■	■	■	■					

GARDEN FLOWERS FOR ARRANGING

Flowering season ▶	early spring	mid-spring	late spring	early summer	mid-summer	late summer	early autumn	mid-autumn	late autumn	early winter	mid-winter	late winter
Clarkia				■	■	■						
Columbine *(Aquilegia)*				■	■	■						
Dahlia				■	■	■	■	■	■			
Dianthus				■	■	■						
Eremurus				■								
Geranium *(Pelargonium)*				■	■	■	■	■				
Gladiolus				■	■	■	■	■	■			
Helichrysum				■	■	■						
Lilies				■	■	■	■	■	■			
Penstemon				■	■							
Peonia				■								
Phlox				■	■	■						
Red hot poker *(Kniphofia)*						■	■					
Salvia				■	■	■						
Sidalcea				■	■	■						
Snapdragon *(Antirrhinum)*				■	■	■						
Sweet peas *(Lathyrus)*				■	■	■						
Nerine								■				

YELLOW TO ORANGE

	early spring	mid-spring	late spring	early summer	mid-summer	late summer	early autumn	mid-autumn	late autumn	early winter	mid-winter	late winter
Crown Imperial *(Fritillaria)*	■	■	■									
Doronicum	■	■	■									
Bulb iris	■	■	■									
Narcissus	■	■	■									
Primulas	■	■	■									
Achillea				■	■	■						
Alstroemeria				■	■	■						
Dahlia				■	■	■	■	■	■			
Bearded iris				■								
Lilies				■	■	■	■	■	■			
Mullein *(Verbascum)*				■	■	■						
Zinnia				■	■	■						
Rudbeckia					■	■	■	■	■			
Crocosmia						■						
Red hot poker *(Kniphofia)*						■	■	■				
Chinese lanterns *(Physalis)*							■	■	■			
Perennial chrysanthemum							■	■	■			
Golden rod *(Solidago)*							■	■	■			

FURTHER READING

FLOWER ARRANGING

The Flower Arranger Editor, Jill Grayson, Little Lions Farm, Ashley Heath, Ringwood, Hants BH24 2EX

Subscriptions Taylor-Bloxham, Nugent Street, Leicester LE3 5HH

The Complete Guide to Foliage and Flower Arrangement – Edited by Iris Webb (*Webb and Bower*)

Flower Decoration – George Smith (*Webb and Bower*)

The Flower Arranger's A-Z – Daphne Vagg (*Batsford*)

GARDENING

Reader's Digest Encyclopaedia of Garden Plants and Flowers

Roses – Roger Phillips and Martyn Rix (*Pan Books*)

Sweet Peas – Your Questions Answered – Charles Unwin (*Unwins seeds*)

The Complete Book of Plant Propagation – Graham Clarke and Alan Toogood (*Ward Lock*)

The Flowering Shrub Expert – Dr. D. G. Hessayon (*Expert Books*)

The Royal Horticultural Society Gardener's Encyclopaedia of Plants and Flowers (Dorling Kindersley)

A Plantsman's Guide to Lilies – Michael Jefferson-Brown (*Ward Lock*)

The Year-Round Bulb Garden – Brian Matthew (*Souvenir Press*)

USEFUL ADDRESSES

SOCIETIES

Royal Horticultural Society's Garden,
Wisley, Woking,
Surrey GU23 6QB

Particulars of membership of the R.H.S. are also available from this address.

City and Guilds of London Institute,
76 Portland Place,
London W1N 4AA

PLANTS AND SEEDS

Bloms Bulbs Ltd.,
Primrose Nursery,
Sharnbrook,
Bedford MK44 1LW

Unwin's Seeds,
Histon,
Cambridge CB4 4ZZ

EQUIPMENT

'Canemates'
6 West Street,
Blandford Forum,
Dorset DT11 7AJ

Hoselock Ltd.,
Haddenham, Aylesbury,
Buckinghamshire

Smithers-Oasis U.K. Ltd.,
14 Tilley Road,
Crowther Ind. Estate,
Washington,
Tyne and Wear NE38 0AE

ACKNOWLEDGEMENTS

I am greatly indebted to Sue Prime, manageress of Greywalls, for her enthusiasm and for all that coffee and delicious shortbread. Without the help and restrained patience of the photographer, Jack Crombie, the book would not have got off the ground. The head gardener at Greywalls, Richard Thorne, grew many of the plants in the flower arrangements and was very good natured about their disappearance from his borders.

For their transparencies,
warmest thanks to: Mike Sleigh – Photographer for the R.H.S.; Unwins Seeds Ltd., Histon, Cambridge; Marie Blom of Bloms Bulbs Ltd., Bedford.

My grateful thanks to: Mr. Alec Mills for all his help with my garden; Drew Miller, Bonnington, for all that cow manure; Joyce Playfair for the arrangement of nerines on page 102; Annie Griffiths for establishing some kind of order.

For allowing me to raid their gardens: Mrs. Anne Gray of Smeaton, East Linton; Mr. and Mrs. Eadie; Mr. Dennis Stewart of the Nether Abbey Hotel, North Berwick; Mr. and Mrs. Wills.

For their advice: Rhona Currie from Flowercraft, Musselburgh; Maxwell Flowers of Edinburgh; George and Isla Craig of St. Andrews; Jill Murdoch, for her inspiration; Amanda Saunders, Unwins Seeds Ltd.; Gem Gardening, Oswaldtwistle, Accrington; Hoselock Ltd.; C. M. Offray (Ribbons), Church Road, Ashford, Middlesex; Stephen Short, Smithers-Oasis, Washington, Tyne and Wear; Alan Shaw, Fison's Horticulture Division, Ipswich; Vitax Ltd., Coalville, Leicester.

And, as always, my love and thanks to my husband, Robbie, for his constant support and his supreme mastery of Microsoft Word.

INDEX

Main references are in **bold** type; *italic* type indicates a reference in the margin